Darwin, Creation and the Fall

Darwin, Creation and the Fall

Theological challenges

Edited by R. J. Berry *and* T. A. Noble

APOLLOS

APOLLOS (an imprint of Inter-Varsity Press)
Norton Street, Nottingham NG7 3HR, England
Email: ivp@ivpbooks.com
Website: www.ivpbooks.com

First published 2009
Reprinted 2010

British Library Cataloguing in Publication Data
A catalogue record for this book is available from the British Library.

ISBN: 978-1-84474-381-0

Set in Monotype Garamond 11/13pt
Typeset in Great Britain by Servis Filmsetting Ltd, Stockport, Cheshire
Printed and bound in Great Britain by Ashford Colour Press Ltd, Gosport,
Hampshire

*Inter-Varsity Press publishes Christian books that are true to the Bible and that communicate
the gospel, develop discipleship and strengthen the church for its mission in the world.*

*Inter-Varsity Press is closely linked with the Universities and Colleges Christian Fellowship,
a student movement connecting Christian Unions in universities and colleges throughout Great
Britain, and a member movement of the International Fellowship of Evangelical Students.
Website: www.uccf.org.uk.*

CONTENTS

CONTRIBUTORS

R. J. (Sam) Berry was Professor of Genetics at University College London 1984–2000. He is a former President of the Linnean Society, British Ecological Society, and Christians in Science. He was Gifford Lecturer in the University of Glasgow 1997–8 (published as *God's Book of Works*, 2003).

Henri Blocher is Professor of Systematic Theology at the Faculté Libre de Théologie Évangélique, Vaux-sur-Seine, near Paris in France and at Wheaton College Graduate School in Illinois. He is President of the Fellowship of European Evangelical Theologians. Among his writings is a trilogy: *In the Beginning* (1984), *Evil and the Cross* (1994) and *Original Sin* (1997).

Darrel Falk is a molecular geneticist, Professor of Biology at Point Loma Nazarene University, in San Diego, California. He is the author of *Coming to Peace with Science: Bridging the Worlds between Faith and Biology* (2004).

Richard S. Hess is Earl S. Kalland Professor of Old Testament and Semitic Languages at Denver Seminary. He is editor of the *Bulletin for Biblical Research* and a prolific author, including *Studies on the Personal Names in Genesis 1–11* (1993, reprinted 2009), *Israelite Religions* (2007) and commentaries on Leviticus, Joshua and the Song of Songs.

A. N. S. Lane is Professor of Historical Theology at London School of Theology. He is the author of *John Calvin: Student of the*

Church Fathers (1999), the *Lion Christian Classics Collection* (2004) and *A Concise History of Christian Thought* (2006). He is a former chairman of the Tyndale Fellowship Christian Doctrine Study Group.

Richard Mortimer is Chaplain to University Centre Hastings, coordinates **the magnet** (a study centre and library run by the Diocese of Chichester) and lectures part-time for the University of Brighton. He has recently completed a PhD investigating different interpretations of the Fall.

T. A. Noble is Senior Research Fellow in Theology at the Nazarene Theological College in Manchester and Professor of Theology at the Nazarene Theological Seminary in Kansas City. He is a former secretary of the Tyndale Fellowship and is chairman of its Christian Doctrine Study Group. He wrote a history of Tyndale House and Fellowship (IVP, 2006), and is one of the editors for the forthcoming revised edition of the IVP *Dictionary of Theology*. He is currently President of the Wesleyan Theological Society (2009–10).

David Wilkinson is Principal of St John's College and Lecturer in the Department of Theology and Religion, University of Durham. He has doctorates in theoretical astrophysics and systematic theology and is a Fellow of the Royal Astronomical Society. He has had a long-standing interest in the relationship between science and religion and is the author of *God, Time and Stephen Hawking* (2001) and *The Message of Creation* (2002) in the Bible Speaks Today series.

ABBREVIATIONS

ANTC	Abingdon New Testament Commentaries
BST	Bible Speaks Today
CD	Karl Barth, *Church Dogmatics*, ed. G. W. Bromiley and T. F. Torrance (ET, Edinburgh: T&T Clark, 1956-75)
JBL	*Journal of Biblical Literature*
JTS	*Journal of Theological Studies*
NICNT	New International Commentary on the NT
NIV	New International Version
NPNF	*Nicene and Post-Nicene Fathers*
NRSV	New Revised Standard Version
REB	Revised English Bible
SJT	*Scottish Journal of Theology*
TNIV	Today's New International Version
TNTC	Tyndale NT commentary
TOTC	Tyndale OT commentary

FOREWORD

The year 2009 is the bicentenary of the birth of Charles Darwin and the one hundred and fiftieth anniversary of the publication of his epoch-making work, *Origin of Species*. Evangelical Christians in particular have debated the extent and mechanisms of evolution, and some hold tenaciously to a complete rejection of Darwin's ideas. But that was not the stance of Evangelical theologians such as James Orr or B. B. Warfield in the decades after Darwin; it was the position adopted by grass-roots fundamentalists in the 1920s in reaction to the way in which T. H. Huxley and others had turned Darwin's science into propaganda for what later came to be called 'Humanism'.[1] Today the heirs of those fundamentalists try to turn the *doctrine* of creation (on which all Christians agree) into a scientific *theory*, so-called 'creationism', which they see as a rival to the neo Darwinian theory of evolution. But they consequently find themselves in disagreement with virtually the whole of modern science, particularly biology, genetics, geology and cosmology.

Those debates are not the subject of this book. Rather, it is an exercise in constructive discussion between science and theology. The eight papers here are written by Evangelical Christians, four theologians and four scientists (one of whom is also a qualified theologian), who accept both the authority of Holy Scripture and

---

1. For fundamentalist rejection of Darwin, see Karl W. Giberson, *Saving Darwin: How to Be a Christian and Believe in Evolution* (New York: HarperCollins, 2008).

the contemporary scientific picture of the world. We believe that, rightly understood, these are not in conflict. That does not mean that we have answers to all the questions which arise, but it does mean that we are prepared to work at resolving apparent conflicts. We proceed in the belief that the universe is the creation of God, but also that it has developed over aeons in the way told by contemporary cosmology. The vastness and unimaginable timescale of the expanding universe only serve to inspire us with greater awe at the majesty and glory of the Creator. If the Lord God is the Creator not of a brief little six-thousand-year-old universe centred on the earth, but of the vast and awe-inspiring beauty of a universe of 13.5 billion years and innumerable galaxies, how much more is his holy name magnified!

Most of the papers in this book focus not so much on the creation as a whole as on the relationship between the story of human origins told by modern science and the story of human origins and of the Fall told in Holy Scripture. 'Is man an ape or an angel?' asked Benjamin Disraeli after the publication of the *Origin*, and answered (as a true politician!), 'I am on the side of the angels.' While none of us wishes to contend that humans are angels, Disraeli's question poses (albeit in rather tendentious terms) the issue we are addressing. How does the Christian doctrine of humanity (what we used to call the doctrine of 'man') as created yet fallen, relate to the biologist's account of the evolution of the human race? If we accept the Darwinian picture of evolution, where does that leave the Christian doctrines of the Fall and of sin? How do we understand 'good' and 'evil'? What basis is there for ethics? And how does this affect the problem of evil and suffering?

Like the doctrine of creation *ex nihilo*, the doctrines of sin and the Fall are integral to Christian theology. Since the Creator cannot be the source of sin and evil, somehow it is because the human race is 'fallen' that there is sin in the world. But many Christian thinkers, particularly since Darwin, have wanted to retain 'fallenness', while dispensing with any event called 'the Fall'. Is that an option for Christian theology? And how would it affect the doctrine of original sin?

The chapters in this volume are edited versions of papers given at meetings of the Christian Doctrine Study Group of the Tyndale

Fellowship on 7–9 July, 2008 and Christians in Science on 1
November, 2008. David Wilkinson fittingly begins by putting the
doctrine of creation in the context of the worship of the Creator.
Theology is never a dispassionate, abstract, neutral discussion
of the latest ideas about a concept we call 'God'. True theology
is always the expression of our personal knowledge within the
believing Church of the One we know as Father through the Son,
Jesus Christ, in the power of the Spirit. It is certainly an intellectual exercise, but one which is only possible by faith within the
worshipping community. R. J. Berry then gives a historical survey
from Darwin's own struggle to relate his science to his faith up to
continuing attempts in the present day to wrestle with the implications of evolution for the Christian understanding of humanity.
This includes his own advocacy of the view that *Homo divinus*
should not be equated simply with *Homo sapiens*. Darrel R. Falk
looks at the theological challenges which arose for Darwin himself,
and asks whether these were in fact new questions or whether the
problems were so intractable for Darwin because he began (like so
many of his generation) with a deist rather than a Christian doctrine of God. Rick Hess then contributes a careful examination of
the text which has so often been at the centre of debate, the early
chapters of Genesis.

T. A. Noble outlines first a clarification of the doctrine of original sin by identifying the different facets of this rather complex
and paradoxical concept, and then attempts to do some fresh
thinking on the doctrine of the Fall, shaped (as all Christian theology should be) in the light of New Testament eschatology. A. N. S.
Lane then takes a close look at the view of the Fall and original sin
taken by Irenaeus, who has sometimes been used (particularly in
recent years by John Hick) as an authority with which to challenge
Augustine. While there are differences, the agreement between the
two Fathers has too often been underplayed. Henri Blocher next
puts us in his debt once again by some critical thinking on some
attempts at theodicy which rationalize evil by denying the reality
of the Fall. He then considers the options if we are to relate the
historicity of Adam to the picture we now have of primeval, pre-
historic humanity. In the final chapter, Richard Mortimer engages
in critically constructive dialogue with Professor Blocher's earlier

writings. As the editors, we then sum up the implications of our discussion in a final Epilogue.

We offer these chapters as pointers to understanding our place and calling in a world where science is constantly changing and frequently challenging our worldview. We follow Jonathan Edwards, one of the strongest champions of biblical orthodoxy, who 'regarded Scripture alone as truly authoritative, so earlier interpreters could be revised'. For Edwards and for us, the project of interpreting Holy Scripture and understanding its true meaning is an ongoing and progressive enterprise.

R. J. Berry
T. A. Noble
Epiphany, 2009

1. WORSHIPPING THE CREATOR GOD: THE CHRISTIAN DOCTRINE OF CREATION

David Wilkinson

The Christian doctrine of creation has too often been highjacked by controversies of creationism, deistic tendencies and a concentration on Genesis 1 to the detriment of the richness of other biblical passages on creation. As a result the discussion of science and religion in the popular arena features Richard Dawkins attacking six-day creationism and the design argument for the existence of God, while many Christians see God the Creator simply as the one who lights the blue touch paper of the Big Bang. Deism, the tendency to see God interacting with the universe only at its very beginning and then going off to watch it from a distance, has been allowed to flourish by separating the doctrine of creation from its foundational scriptures.

What does it mean to take the Bible seriously in this area and in particular to take the whole of the Bible seriously? It is very tempting to construct a doctrine of creation from just the Old Testament texts,[1] but in doing so one misses the major Christian

---

1. D. Wilkinson, 'Creation Accounts in the Old Testament', in N. Spurway

themes of creation seen in the light of new creation, and a God who sustains every moment of the universe's existence in Jesus.

Recapturing a Christian doctrine of creation from Scripture allows us to move beyond the controversies of creationism and encounter a fruitful dialogue with science. Perhaps more importantly it also leads to an emphasis that the most important insight into creation is the Creator God who is to be worshipped, enjoyed and trusted.

In order to help us into this way of thinking I therefore turn to Colossians 1:15–20, rather than Genesis 1, as a key passage to hold us to a Christian doctrine of creation. This allows us to suggest the following framework.

The Christian doctrine of creation is never an abstract academic concept

Scripture is of course extremely rich in a diversity of styles as it discusses creation.[2] Even within the Old Testament, a first reading of Proverbs 8:22–31, Psalms 8, 19 and 148, Genesis 9:8–17, Job 38:1 – 41:34 and Isaiah 40:9–31 shows very different styles represented by both wisdom and prophetic traditions. In Genesis 1 – 3 we note the differences of styles of Genesis 1:1 – 2:4 and Genesis 2:4 – 3:24. This diversity in the way the biblical writers discuss and present creation is a reminder of just how rich the doctrine is but also that it is a dynamic and practical doctrine. The Bible never discusses creation in terms of cosmology for its own sake but in order to inspire worship, to encourage the weak, to call for holiness, and to offer reassurance in times of trouble.

Colossians 1:15–20 illustrates this. It has long been recognized that this passage is carefully worded and rhythmically balanced

---

Footnote 1 (*cont.*)

(ed.), *Creation and the Abrahamic Faiths* (Newcastle: Cambridge Scholar's Press, 2008), pp. 1–12.

2. For a detailed exposition of these passages see D. Wilkinson, *The Message of Creation* (Leicester: IVP, 2002).

with a number of significant repetitions and parallels. Some scholars have suggested that it is a Christian poem, or it could even be an early hymn. Since the time of Eduard Norden in 1923 scholars have been happy to believe that Paul borrowed an already-existing piece of a hymn or liturgy.[3] The truth is that there is not enough information for us to be sure of its original setting; but this does not affect our understanding about how Paul used this passage.

Paul is responding to groups either inside or outside of the young church who were saying that Jesus is not that special. It is difficult to know where this was coming from. Dunn has suggested that there may have been a diffuse series of groups and ideas rather than one heretical stance.[4] Some have suggested that the problem in the church was gnosticizing syncretism, where beliefs in intermediate cosmic powers and mystery cult initiation rites were being grafted into the Christian faith. Others have argued that the problem stemmed from Jewish synagogues as the source of influences that threatened the church, which attempted to force Christian converts to 'complete' their faith by becoming Jews.[5]

The truth may be that all these elements were at work. Notwithstanding, Paul's response is clear. He identifies a common theme within all of these tendencies, the message 'Jesus is *not* that special.' False teachers were saying to the young Christians that they needed more than Jesus in order to be really Christians, whether this be secret rites or secret knowledge. Indeed the absence of polemic in Paul's response may indicate an even more fundamental danger than obvious theological heresy. That could have been that Christ's status and significance were being devalued rather than attacked and an alternative religious system was being subtly exalted. Paul saw the great danger in this because it misunderstood who Jesus was and what faith in him implied. So Paul reminds the

---

3. E. Norden, *Agnostos Theos: Untersuchungen zur Formengeschichte Religiöser Rede* (Darmstadt: Wissenschaftliche Buchgesellschaft, 1956 [1923]).

4. J. D. G. Dunn, *The Epistles to the Colossians and to Philemon* (Carlisle: Paternoster, 1996), p. 76.

5. See for example N. T. Wright, *Colossians and Philemon* (TNTC; Leicester: IVP, 1986).

young Christians in Colossae of who Jesus is by painting a majestic picture of Christ in relation to creation and new creation.

Here a passage on creation is being used not in the abstract, but as a way to combat error and indeed to excite Christians again about Jesus. Whether or not this passage was used as a hymn in the early Christian community, a sense of worship runs through it. In a similar way when we come to Genesis 1, there is good reason to see this passage as a hymn or liturgy, with the writer far more concerned about getting the reader to worship this amazing Creator God rather than with the mechanics of how God did it.

Dan Hardy has argued that at its heart the action of God in creation requires worship.[6] The call to worship is written into the very fabric of the universe. In the light of this, we need therefore as Christians to be extremely wary of letting discussion of creation move too far away from its implications for worship and lifestyle. This does not mean that the Christian will not be an enthusiastic and active participant in science and cosmology, but it does mean that the scientific exploration of origins is not to be an end in itself. Put another way, we need to be very careful to focus on the Creator, not just on creation itself.

The Christian doctrine of creation has Christ at the centre

Focusing on the Creator poses the fundamental question of how that Creator is known. Paul is explicit in saying that the Creator God is known supremely in Christ. Jesus is the 'image of the invisible God' (v. 15), the projection of God himself into the dimensions of space-time in a way that reveals his true nature. In answer to the question of how the Creator is known, Christians respond that he is known through his revelation in Jesus Christ.

Later in the passage Paul claims that in Jesus 'God was pleased to have all his fullness dwell' (v. 19[7]), or as N. T. Wright trans-

---

6. D. W. Hardy, *God's Ways with the World* (Edinburgh: T&T Clark, 1996), p. 157.

7. All Bible quotations unless otherwise indicated are TNIV.

lates it, 'God in all his fullness was pleased to take up permanent residence in him'.[8] Paul re-emphasizes such an understanding in Colossians 2:9, 'It is in him that all the fullness of deity dwells in bodily form'. Does that mean that Jesus was fully God but not really human, as if God came to earth just with the outward appearance of humanity? Paul will not allow that; he insists on both full divinity and full humanity through reference to the physical body (v. 22) and 'bodily form' (Col. 2:9).

As we celebrate the achievements of Darwin, this insight from the Christian doctrine of creation becomes extremely important. As I have argued elsewhere, the force of Darwin hit not on the questioning of the literal truth of Genesis 1 (as many Christians in the nineteenth century did not hold to a 6,000-year-old creation) but on a view of human uniqueness and more particularly on the design argument.[9] By providing an alternative explanation through natural selection, Darwin showed that the design argument as a logical proof of the existence of God did not work. Thus the shift from revelation to reason in the nineteenth century, characterized by the exaltation of the design argument over biblical revelation, meant that Darwin became a major threat to some religious believers. As David Livingstone has pointed out, it is interesting that those who held most firmly to a strong doctrine of providence as seen in the biblical revelation (such as B. B. Warfield) had fewer problems with evolution.[10]

In the twentieth century, the centrality of Christ to the doctrine of creation was represented forcibly in the thinking of Karl Barth. For Barth, God's self-disclosure in Jesus of Nazareth is essential even to understanding aright what it means to view God as creator:

---

8. Wright, *Colossians and Philemon*, p. 23–30, n. 5.

9. D. Wilkinson, 'Reading Genesis in the Light of Modern Science', in S. Barton and D. Wilkinson (eds.), *Reading Genesis After Darwin* (New York: OUP, 2009).

10. D. Livingstone, *Darwin's Forgotten Defenders* (Edinburgh: Scottish Academic Press, 1987).

I believe in Jesus Christ, God's Son our Lord, in order to perceive and
to understand that God the Almighty, the Father, is Creator of heaven
and earth. If I did not believe the former, I could not perceive and
understand the latter.[11]

That is why Dawkins is completely correct in showing that his
'God hypothesis' is a delusion.[12] He refuses to engage with any particular expression of religious belief or revelation and defines the
hypothesis of God in the broadest possible sense. He then goes on
to show that the design and cosmological arguments do not work.
None of this should be a surprise to a Christian holding a biblical
doctrine of creation. The universe cannot be fully understood as
creation without Christ. Indeed the main Christian critique of the
Dawkins approach is how little attention he gives to any discussion of the life, death and resurrection of Jesus.

At this point a word of caution is important to Christians who
want to push six-day creationism or intelligent design as apologetic
strategies. Some six-day creationists attempt to demonstrate that
modern science is wrong and there are strong scientific arguments
for accepting the literal truth of Genesis 1. Some then seem to go
on and say, 'Now that I have proved Genesis is correct, then the
whole of the Bible follows'. Alternatively, 'intelligent design' argues
that science is incomplete in its description of the development of
the universe, and that only the intervention of an intelligence can
explain the development of complexity. There are key questions
here for Evangelical Christians concerning whether six-day creationism is the best interpretation of the Genesis narratives, and
whether intelligent design is good science.[13] Any apologetic strategy which stems from the Christian doctrine of creation must have
a key place for Jesus. I remain unconvinced that many forms of
six-day creationism or intelligent design sufficiently represent the
centrality of Christ.

---

11. K. Barth, *CD* vol. III, p. 29.

12. R. Dawkins, *The God Delusion* (London: Bantam Press, 2006), p. 31.

13. Denis Alexander, *Creation or Evolution – Do We Have to Choose?* (Oxford:
    Monarch, 2008).

Is there therefore nothing to be said about the Creator God outside of God's revelation in Jesus? What about the concept of natural theology, wherein the universe might give us knowledge of God? Barth famously said a big 'no' to natural theology, but we need not go that far. First we need to take seriously that 'the heavens declare the glory of God' (Ps. 19:1). God may choose to reveal himself through the natural world, through the book of his works as well as through the book of his word. Secondly, the Christian doctrine of creation says that natural theology and revealed theology should always be held together.

An interesting example of this approach can be seen back in the nineteenth century. In 1835 Rev. Temple Chevalier was invited to become Professor of Mathematics at the newly founded University of Durham. Subsequently he also became Reader in Hebrew, and in 1841 its first Professor of Astronomy. In his Cambridge Hulsean Lectures, 'On the proofs of Divine Power and Wisdom, derived from the study of astronomy and the evidence, doctrines and precepts of Revealed Religion' (1827), he uses twelve sermons modelled on the structure of Psalm 19 to give 'the evidence for revealed religion'. The first four look at evidence from astronomy, the next four are on the Bible and the last four on the spiritual life. Chevalier is interesting for a number of reasons. Three decades before the publication of the *Origin*, he demonstrates the commitment of both a scientist and an ordained clergyman, and in the heyday of natural theology he shows a commitment to the importance of revelation. Further, 'proofs of Divine Power' are not for Chevalier philosophical arguments leading to a logical proof of the existence of God. They are rather scientific pointers or questions which can only be interpreted correctly in Jesus. Some of these pointers concern the 'wow' of the size of the universe or the beauty of the mathematical laws.

This approach is quite different from intelligent design. It does not look for gaps within the scientific account into which God has to be squeezed as the only explanation. It looks at the scientific description of the world as a whole, allows science to raise questions such as the intelligibility of the universe or the origin of the laws of physics, which lie beyond science's ability to answer, and sees these questions from a framework of a Creator God who reveals himself in Jesus. It is an approach seen not only in the nineteenth century in Chevalier but in a number of Christians contributing to the dialogue of science and religion today.[14]

The Christian doctrine of creation affirms that God is the sole creator of the universe

The doctrine of creation affirms that the universe cannot be fully understood without reference to God. The Christian doctrine of creation goes further and locates creation in the action of God in Christ. C. F. Burney argued that in the Colossians passage, Paul echoes the understanding of 'wisdom' in the Old Testament, where God creates the world through wisdom.[15] For Paul the creative work of God is expressed not through a concept or indeed a personification of a divine attribute or holy law but through the person of Jesus Christ.

First, this cosmic picture of Jesus conveys that God is the source of all creation. To say that Christ is 'the firstborn over all creation' (v. 15) is not meant to imply that Jesus was himself created. The idea is of priority in both time and rank, or as F. F. Bruce translates,[16] 'firstborn *before* all creation'. Then Paul gets carried away with excitement as he describes the creative work of Jesus. All things were created by/in him (v. 16), by/through him (v. 16b), and for him (v. 16b). He is therefore the foundation, the agent and the goal of creation. This is a big picture of Jesus and creation.

It is at this point we may be reminded by J. B. Phillips that 'Your God is too small'. The Christian doctrine of creation continually challenges us to take seriously the greatness of God and the

---

14. E.g. J. Polkinghorne, *Theology in the Context of Science* (SPCK: London, 2008).

15. C. F. Burney, 'Christ as the APXH of Creation', *JTS* 27 (1926), pp. 160–177.

16. F. F. Bruce, *The Epistles to the Colossians, to Philemon and to the Ephesians* (NICNT; Grand Rapids: Eerdmans, 1984), p. 59.

wonder of such a creation. It is interesting that in *The God Delusion* Dawkins quotes some famous words from Carl Sagan in order to attack religious believers:

> How is it that hardly any major religion has looked at science and concluded, 'This is better than we thought! The universe is much bigger than our prophets said, grander, more subtle, more elegant'? Instead they say, 'No, no, no! My god is a little god, and I want him to stay that way'. A religion, old or new, that stressed the magnificence of the universe as revealed by modern science might be able to draw forth reserves of reverence and awe hardly tapped by the conventional faiths.[17]

Christians have looked at the universe and indeed should look at it, with awe and excitement, and with the sense that God, who became a human being in Jesus, is the amazing Creator of 100 billion stars in each of 100 billion galaxies. Science, whether it be through Stephen Hawking or Charles Darwin, allows us to see just how great God is.

The belief that God is the source of all creation has been developed theologically into *creatio ex nihilo*, that is, creation out of nothing. Some have argued that the biblical material is at best ambiguous as to whether God simply shaped the universe from pre-existing matter, somewhat like an architect imposing order on matter, and that creation out of nothing only came to clear articulation as the Christian faith encountered and responded to the questions and challenges of Greek philosophy and Gnostic thought.[18] I do not believe that the early chapters of Genesis are as ambiguous on this as some would think. Certainly the New Testament is unequivocal in its belief that all that exists has its source in nothing other than the limitless possibilities for life that God is (John 1:3; Col. 1:16; Heb. 1:3).

---

17. C. Sagan, *Pale Blue Dot* (New York: Ballantine Books, 1994), p. 52.
18. G. May, *Creatio Ex Nihilo: The Doctrine of 'Creation out of Nothing' in Early Christian Thought* (Edinburgh: University of Edinburgh Press, 1994); F. Young, 'Creatio ex nihilo: A Context for the Emergence of the Christian Doctrine of Creation', *SJT* 44 (1991), p. 141.

It is important to recognize that if the whole material universe is created by God, then the natural sciences are affirmed. Indeed many historians of science would say that the Christian doctrine of creation was of prime importance in the development of modern science.[19] Creation is both to be valued rather than to be escaped, and free to be investigated rather than worshipped. Along with this, God was not constrained in creating by the limitations of pre-existing matter but could create freely. Thus, to understand fully the God-given order of the universe it is necessary to observe it, which is the basic principle of empirical science.

Second, this cosmic picture of Jesus suggests that God is the sustainer of order in creation. Paul in verse 17 of Colossians 1 reminds us that Christ is before all things, but also that 'in him all things hold together'. This is a very different picture from the deistic Creator who lights the blue touch paper of the Big Bang and then goes off to have a cup of tea! The Creator God is the sustainer of creation. The verb is in the perfect indicating everything held together in him and continues so to do.

As an astrophysicist this has always been an important verse for me. The simplicity of the physical laws underlying the complexity of the universe is one of the striking features of modern science. The fact the universe 'holds together' or 'coheres' in such an amazing way is not only because of an impersonal physical theory but because of the creative work of Jesus. Science is only possible because of the work of Jesus.

The Christian doctrine of creation affirms science and technology by seeing them as gifts of God. Those who explore the order of the universe such as scientists, or those who exploit the order such as engineers, do so because of God, whether they recognize it or not. In that way, science, engineering and technology are Christian ministries. So Kepler in 1595 wrote to Maestlin, one of his teachers, that he did not regret turning away from a vocation as a theologian and that 'through my effort God is being celebrated

---

19. P. Harrison, *The Bible, Protestantism and the Rise of Natural Science* (Cambridge: CUP, 1998).

in astronomy'.[20] Likewise we need to encourage Christian believers to see science as a Christian vocation rather than a secular threat.

The Christian doctrine of creation needs to be seen in the light of the reality of new creation

For Paul the supremacy of Christ is seen not just in creation but also in new creation. In order to show this Paul uses parallels within the passage to stress the supremacy of Christ in both creation and new creation:[21]

- he is the image of the invisible God (v. 15a) and the beginning (v. 18b);
- he is the 'firstborn' of all creation (v. 15b) and from the dead (v. 18c);
- he is pre-eminent, as he is before all things (v. 17a) and head of the church, the beginning and firstborn (v. 18);
- the Son unifies, as in him all things hold together (v. 17b) and he reconciles all things (v. 20a);
- everything is related to him in creation (v. 16b) and in new creation (v. 20c).

In addition the sequence of 'in him . . . through him . . . to him. . .' is paralleled in both verses 16 and 19–20a, implying that the same agent accomplishes both creation and new creation. Jesus is not simply an historical human being or even a mediator of present religious experience: he is both Lord of creation and new creation.

The parallels link creation and new creation. The one who is Creator is also Redeemer. The agent of creation is also the goal

20. O. Gingerich, *The Eye of Heaven: Ptolemy, Copernicus, Kepler* (New York: American Institute of Physics, 1993), p. 307.

21. J. M. Robinson, 'A Formal Analysis of Colossians 1:15–20', *JBL* 76 (1957), pp. 270–287; M. Hay, *Colossians* (ANTC; Nashville: Abingdon Press, 2000).

to which the creation tends, its eschatological purpose. Of course this is based in the Old Testament view that Israel's God, the one who delivered them from Egypt, is also the Creator of the whole universe (Isa. 40:12–31).

One of the key aspects of this new creation is reconciliation. Sin is overcome by Jesus' death on the cross and Paul's use of 'blood' (v. 20) gives a model for this reconciliation in the idea of sacrifice. However, his canvas is large. Another parallel between the One who creates 'all things' and reconciles 'all things' emphasizes the universal scope of God's action. In fact this is further emphasized by yet another parallel between verses 19 and 20. His argument is that because 'the fullness' of God was in Christ then there will be a fullness of 'all things' redeemed. The image of reconciliation also has the sense of bringing the entire universe into a new order and harmony, a fulfilment of God's plan for it.[22]

At the heart of the parallels is the phrase 'firstborn'. It is used as 'over all creation' (v. 15) and then 'from the dead' (v. 18). Jesus is not only the beginning of the creation; he is also the beginning of the new creation. This is demonstrated by his resurrection. His resurrection is the beginning not only of the new age, but will be followed by the resurrection of believers.

Therefore, in the many parallels that the writer uses, we see again the centrality of Christ, and we have a clear understanding of the link between the resurrection of Jesus and the reconciliation of all things. As Wright puts it, 'with the resurrection itself, a shock wave has gone through the entire cosmos: the new creation has been born, and must now be implemented'.[23] But we may ask, what does it really mean for a shock wave to go through the entire cosmos? In what sense is the new creation born? Perhaps the image of birth is not a bad image in this context. The birth of a child is a dramatic event which has both immediate effects and points forward to a new phase of family life. We can see the pointers to the future in the resurrection. But what are the immediate

---

22. Wright, *Colossians and Philemon*, p. 68 (see n. 2).
23. N.T. Wright, *The Resurrection of the Son of God* (London: SPCK, 2003), p. 239.

effects of the resurrection on this creation? The Gospel writers interestingly enough see little immediate effects on creation in the aftermath of the resurrection. Indeed, Matthew's earthquake and associated upheavals happen at the death of Jesus (Matt. 27:51–53). The immediate effects are of course on transformed, hopeful and puzzled people. The birth of the new creation is seen in the power of the gospel to change lives. However, the dramatic and immediate effects should not blind us to the longer-term consequences. The Christian doctrine of creation always asks us to expand our horizon in these consequences.

The Christian doctrine of creation maintains that this creation really is good, whilst also looking forward in the purposes of God to a new creation, a 'new heaven and new earth' (Rev. 21). The hope is not of God completely starting again, or the hope for some kind of disembodied immaterial state, but the hope for the transfiguring fulfillment of this present creation into all that it was called into being to be. Given this combination of identity and transformation, the present created order is not to be written off as evil or unimportant, but is, rather, to be cared for, respected, enjoyed and delighted in.

The Christian doctrine of creation sees humanity as the gift of intimate relationship with God

The question of what it means to be human is one of the central questions of contemporary culture. Advances in artificial intelligence, the Human Genome Project, the nature of the human brain and greater understandings of the capabilities of animals, all push the question of what is special about human beings. Traditional theological thinking has often attempted to define the unique nature of human beings as their possession of an immaterial soul or by attempting to define the image of God.

While the main focus of this Colossians passage is on Jesus, the reader will be drawn to think about the nature of humanity by Paul's use of 'image of God', reminding us of the Genesis text where men and women are made in the image of God (Gen. 1:27). The meaning of 'image' has caused considerable debate. Different suggestions have included that God is physically embodied and human beings are physically the image of God; that the image denotes human reason; freedom; or our moral sense. Yet none of these interpretations does justice to the biblical material. Studies in the language and context of the ancient Near East lead to a different understanding of image as not so much a part of the human constitution as a pointer to the distinctive place of humanity within the created order. It is less about something we have or do and more about relationship.[24]

In contrast to the Babylonian account where the role of humans is simply one of serving the gods, humanity is viewed here, in distinction from the rest of creaturely reality, as enjoying a relationship of unique conscious intimacy with God. Or, perhaps better, humanity is that part of creation that is capable of being conscious of and responsive in its relationship to the Creator. As David Fergusson has put it, 'The image of God is thus to be understood not substantively in terms of the possession of an immortal soul, but relationally in terms of the role that human beings play before God and before the rest of creation.'[25] Furthermore, as this already implies, this relationship involves responsibility. In particular, there is a close connection in the text between being made in the image of God and God's command to humans to exercise dominion over the natural world (Gen. 1:26–28). This is to be understood as a call to share in the creative, sustaining dominion of God and so act as the visible representatives of God's benevolent care for creation.

In this context it is significant that it is Jesus of Nazareth who is *the* disclosure par excellence of true divine power in a manner profoundly subversive of common expectations and, likewise, Jesus who is regarded as truly being in the 'image of God'. Thus we see not only what God is like in Jesus, we also see what human beings are meant to be.

Therefore if being made in the image of God involves responsibility and stewardship of the natural world, we need to exercise

---

24. C. Westermann, *Genesis 1–11*, vol. 1 (London: SPCK, 1984), p. 158.
25. David Fergusson, *The Cosmos and the Creator* (London: SPCK, 1998), p. 14.

that responsibility in a Christ-like way, as servant rather than as ruthless dictator. This is an added dimension to thinking about our response to the environmental crisis. As Christians we share the concern for the environment that future generations will have to live with, we share with other faith communities the sense of caring for the Earth as creation, but we also want to go further and see environmental responsibility as part of living under the lordship of Christ.

It is striking that the Genesis 1 narrative reaches fulfillment not in the creation of Adam and Eve but in the sabbath day on which 'the whole creation glorifies its maker'.[26] This provides further perspective on the distinctive role of humans within the created order as that of priests giving voice to creation's praise. That is, resting in, rejoicing in and living out of the sabbath praise of God is regarded here as the very pinnacle of what created reality and human reality in particular is called to. Viewed in this way, we humans are called not just to 'use' material reality for our own ends, but to hallow it, to reverence it as God's gift, to work for its flourishing and, in this manner, be viceroys of God's gracious generative sovereignty in God's good world.

We have therefore reviewed the Christian doctrine of creation and found a common theme. The meaning of the universe is not to be found in an impersonal cosmic force, or in a mathematical theory of everything, or in an abstract philosophical idea, but in a personal God who wants to be in relationship with human beings. To be human is to be given the gift of relationship, to love and to be loved by the God who created you.

The Christian doctrine of creation points us to the God of creation who is revealed in Jesus Christ, and calls us to worship God through the way we think, act and live.

© David Wilkinson, 2009

---

26. Ibid., p. 17.

2. DID DARWIN DETHRONE HUMANKIND?

R. J. Berry

The two books for which Charles Darwin is best known (*Origin of Species*, 1859 and *Descent of Man,* 1871) raised unavoidable theological questions about humankind. Peter Bowler put the challenges starkly:

> If Christians accepted that humanity was the product of evolution – even assuming the process could be seen as an expression of the Creator's will – then the whole idea of Original Sin would have to be reinterpreted. Far from falling from an original state of grace in the Garden of Eden, we have risen gradually from our animal origins. And if there was no Sin from which we needed salvation, what was the purpose of Christ's agony on the cross? Christ became merely the perfect man who showed us what we could all hope to become when evolution finished its upward course. Small wonder that many conservative Christians – and not just the American fundamentalists – argued that such a transformation had destroyed the very foundations of their faith.[1]

---

1. Peter Bowler, *Monkey Trials and Gorilla Sermons* (Cambridge, MA: Harvard University Press, 2007), p. 7.

Thomas Henry Huxley, Darwin's 'bulldog', notoriously wrote, 'Exhausted theologians lie about the cradle of every science as the strangled snakes beside that of Hercules; and history records that wherever science and orthodoxy have been fairly opposed, the latter has been forced to retire from the lists, bleeding and crushed if not annihilated; scotched if not slain.'[2] Intriguingly, the same bruiser wrote later in life:

> It is the secret of the best theological teachers to the majority of their opponents that they substantially recognize the realities of things, however strange the forms in which they clothe their conceptions. The doctrines of predestination; of original sin; of the innate depravity of man and the evil fate of the greater part of the human race; of the primacy of Satan in this world, faulty as they are, appear to me to be vastly nearer the truth than the 'liberal' popular illusions that babes are all born good and that the example of a corrupt society is responsible for their failure to remain so; that it is given to everybody to reach the ethical ideal if he will only try. . .[3]

What is the right way to react to Darwin and the *Origin of Species?* There have been many attempts to summarize and generalize.[4] An early response was from Adam Sedgwick, Darwin's teacher and Professor of Geology at Cambridge University. He reviewed the *Origin* in the *Spectator:*

> I have read Darwin's book. It is clever and calmly written; and therefore the more mischievous if its principles be false; and I believe them *utterly*

---

2. T. H. Huxley, *Collected Essays. Darwinia* (London, 1896), p. 52.

3. T. H. Huxley, 'An Apologetic Irenicon', *Fortnightly Review* n.s. 52 (1892), pp. 557–571; p. 569.

4. For example, D. L. Hull, *Darwin and his Critics* (Chicago: Chicago University Press, 1973); J. R. Moore, *The Post-Darwinian Controversies* (Cambridge: Cambridge University Press, 1979). The two definitive accounts of Darwin's life are: A. Desmond and J. R. Moore, *Darwin* (London: Michael Joseph, 1991); J. Moore, *Charles Darwin* (London: Jonathan Cape, 1995, 2002).

false . . . It repudiates all reasoning from final causes; and seems to
shut the door upon any view (however feeble) of the God of Nature
as manifested in His works. From first to last it is a dish of rank
materialism cleverly cooked and served up . . . And why is this done?
For no other solid reason, I am sure, except to make us independent of
a Creator.[5]

Perhaps the most serious concern about Darwin's thesis was –
and is – that the universe might be governed by chance rather than
God. This becomes particularly critical if it applies to humankind.
Is the appearance of humans on earth simply fortuitous? Is there
anything special about us? Are we no more than animals? A century
before Darwin, Linnaeus had classified mankind in the same group
as the great apes. In contrast, a few decades later, the French palae-
ontologist, Baron Cuvier, regarded our species as so distinct from the
other animals that he did not expect that human fossils would exist.[6]
Darwin himself noted as early as 1838, 'Man in his arrogance thinks
himself a great work worthy of the interposition of a deity. More
humble & I think truer to consider him created from animals.'[7]
Assumptions about the status of humankind changed significantly following the Enlightenment. An indication of this was
when in 1691, John Ray wrote in *The Wisdom of God Manifested in
the Works of Creation* that 'It is a generally received opinion that all
this visible world was created for Man . . . yet wise men nowadays
think otherwise'. Reviewing the post-Enlightenment period, Keith
Thomas judged that 'at the start of the early modern period, man's
ascendancy over the natural world was the unquestioned object
of human endeavour. By 1800 it was still the aim of most people
. . . but by this time the objective was no longer unquestioned'.[8]

---

5. A. Sedgwick, 'Objections to Mr. Darwin's Theory of the Origin of
   Species', *Spectator* (24 March 1860), pp. 285–286; ibid. (7 April 1860),
   pp. 334–335, p. 334.
6. E. Mayr, *The Growth of Biological Thought* (Cambridge, MA: Belknap Press,
   1982).
7. *Bulletin of the British Museum* (Natural History), Historical Series 2, 1960.
8. Keith Thomas, *Man and the Natural World* (London: Allen Lane, 1983), p. 242.

The implications of this were uncomfortable. Don Cupitt has described the situation:

> Mechanistic science was allowed to explain the structure and workings of physical nature without restriction. But who designed this beautiful world-machine and set it going in the first place? Only Scripture could answer that question. So science dealt with the everyday tick-tock of the cosmic framework and religion dealt with the ultimates: first beginnings and last ends, God and the soul . . . It was a happy compromise while it lasted. Science promoted the cause of religion by showing the beautiful workmanship of the world . . . But there was a fatal flaw in the synthesis. Religious ideas were being used to plug the gaps in scientific theory. Science could not yet explain how animals and plants had originated and had become so wonderfully adapted to their environment so that was handed over to religion. People still made a sharp soul-body distinction and the soul fell beyond the scope of science – so everything to do with human inwardness and personal and social behaviour remained the province of the preacher and moralist.[9]

And then came Darwin, providing an easily understood way of how the world could come into being without supernatural agency. As Richard Dawkins put it, 'although atheism might have been tenable before Darwin, Darwin made it possible to be an intellectually fulfilled atheist'.[10] Is Charles Darwin the anti-Christ? Or did Oxford theologian Aubrey Moore get it right when he wrote a generation after the *Origin of Species* that Darwin did the work of a friend under the guise of a foe by making it impossible to accept the image of an occasionally interfering absentee landlord?[11] For Moore, Darwinism:

---

9. Don Cupitt, *The Sea of Faith* (London: BBC, 1984), p. 59. Writing from the standpoint of a historian, John Greene has reviewed the events between John Ray and Charles Darwin as *The Death of Adam. Evolution and Its Impact on Western Thought* (Ames: Iowa State University Press, 1959).

10. Richard Dawkins, *The Blind Watchmaker* (London: Longman, 1986), p. 6.

11. A. Moore, 'The Christian Doctrine of God', in C. Gore (ed.), *Lux Mundi* (London: John Murray, 1889), p. 99.

is infinitely more Christian than the theory of 'special creation' for it implies the immanence of God in nature, and the omnipresence of His creative power . . . Deism, even when it struggled to be orthodox, constantly spoke of God as we might speak of an absentee landlord, who cares nothing for his property so long as he gets his rent. Yet nothing more opposed to the language of the Bible and the Fathers can hardly be imagined . . . For Christians the *facts of nature* are *the acts of God*. Religion relates these facts to God as their Author, science relates them to one another as integral parts of a visible order. Religion does not tell us of their interrelations, science cannot speak of their relation to God. Yet the religious view of the world is infinitely deepened and enriched when we not only recognize it as the work of God but are able to trace the relation of part to part.[12]

Charles Darwin was born in Shrewsbury on 12 February 1809, the same day as Abraham Lincoln. Lincoln became a leader in slave liberation; if Moore is right, perhaps it is not too fanciful to think of Darwin as a liberator as well – freeing both scientists and theologians from the constraints of outdated views about God and nature. By destroying the credibility of post-Enlightenment Deism he potentially revolutionized theology as much as science.

Darwin followed his father and elder brother to medical school in Edinburgh (1825–7), but found himself too squeamish for a medical career. He transferred to Cambridge, reading for a general degree (1828–31), and followed this by five much more exciting years (1832–6) as a 'gentleman naturalist' on *HMS Beagle*, commissioned under the command of Robert Fitzroy to survey the southern coasts of South America. The *Beagle* went on to circumnavigate the globe, most famously spending three weeks (16 September to 20 October 1835) around the islands of the equatorial Galapagos Archipelago, 1,000 km west of the South American mainland.

Darwin never left Britain again. His scientific reputation was made by his account of the *Voyage of the Beagle*, published in 1839.

---

12. A. Moore, *Science and the Faith* (London: Kegan Paul, Trench, Trübner, 1892), p. 184–185.

In the same year he was elected a Fellow of the Royal Society and married his cousin, Emma Wedgwood (granddaughter of the founder of the Wedgwood pottery firm). The couple lived first in London (in a house where the Biology Department of University College London now stands) and then at Down House near Bromley in Kent until their respective deaths – Charles in 1882 and Emma in 1896.

Darwin's assumption had been that he would seek ordination after his Cambridge degree. He wrote home at an early stage of the *Beagle*'s voyage, 'Although I like this knocking about, I find I steadily have a distant prospect of a very quiet parsonage & I can see it even through a grove of Palms.' After leaving Edinburgh, he had read with approval the evangelical Bishop of Chester's *Evidences of Christianity*.[13] At Cambridge, he was required to study William Paley's *Evidences of Christianity*;[14] he found Paley's logic 'irresistible'. In his *Autobiography* he notes, 'The logic of this book and I may add of his *Natural Theology* gave me as much delight as did Euclid. The careful study of these works . . . was the only part of the Academic Course which, as I then felt and still believe, was of the least use to me in the education of my mind.'[15]

But during his time on the *Beagle*, he began to drift away from the idea of a career as a clergyman. He did not become an atheist; in his *Autobiography*, he insisted that he continued to believe in some form of God after his return. Notwithstanding, as Janet Browne comments,

It is clear that his kind of belief, though orthodox, was a very loose, English-style orthodoxy in which it was far less trouble to believe than it was to disbelieve . . . For Darwin, as for countless others, belonging to the Church of England was as much a statement of social position and attitude than it was a profession of any particular doctrine . . . No sane

---

13. J. B. Sumner, *Evidences of Christianity derived from its Nature and Reception* (London, 1821). Sumner was Archbishop of Canterbury 1848–62.

14. W. Paley, *Evidences of Christianity* (London, 1802).

15. N. Barlow (ed.), *The Autobiography of Charles Darwin, 1809–1882, with original omissions restored* (London: Collins, 1958), p. 59.

man could believe in miracles, he decided . . . Yet he went to church regularly throughout the voyage, attending the shipboard ceremonies conducted by Fitzroy and services on shore whenever possible.[16]

Many years later he commented, 'My theology is a simple muddle. I cannot look at the universe as a result of blind chance, yet I can see no evidence of beneficent design, or indeed a design of any kind in the details.'[17] Certainly he was much affected by the death in 1851 of his adored 10-year-old daughter Annie.

A major stumbling-block for Darwin was animal suffering. He wrote (22 May 1860) to his Christian friend, Asa Gray, Professor of Botany at Harvard,

> I own that I cannot see, as plainly as others do & as I shd wish to
> do, evidence of design & beneficence on all sides of us. There seems
> to me too much misery in the world. I cannot persuade myself that
> a beneficent & omnipotent God would have designedly created the
> Ichneumonidæ with the express intention of their feeding within the
> living bodies of caterpillars, or that a cat should play with mice. Not
> believing this, I see no necessity in the belief that the eye was expressly
> designed. On the other hand I cannot anyhow be contented to view this
> wonderful universe & especially the nature of man, & to conclude that
> everything is the result of brute force. I am inclined to look at everything
> as resulting from designed laws, with the details, whether good or bad,
> left to the working out of what we may call chance.[18] Not that this

---

16. Janet Browne, *Charles Darwin. Voyaging* (London: Jonathan Cape, 1995), p. 325.

17. Letter to J. D. Hooker, 12 July 1870. This issue is discussed in more detail by Darrel Falk in ch. 3 of this volume, pp. 76f.

18. He concluded the *Origin*: 'It is interesting to contemplate a tangled bank, clothed with many plants of many kinds, with birds singing on the bushes, with various insects flitting about, and with worms crawling through the damp earth, and to reflect that these elaborately constructed forms, so different from each other and dependent upon each other in so complex a manner, have all been produced by laws acting around us . . . From the war of nature, from famine and death, the most exalted

notion *at all* satisfies me. I feel most deeply that the whole subject is too profound for the human intellect . . . I can see no reason, why a man, or other animal, may not have been aboriginally produced by other laws; & that all these laws may have been expressly designed by an omniscient Creator, who foresaw every future event & consequence. But the more I think the more bewildered I become.

One assertion that is certainly not true is the story often repeated in some evangelical circles that Darwin underwent a death-bed conversion. The source and embroidering of this tale has been refuted in detail as a 'grotesque gloss on real historical events' by Jim Moore.[19]

William Phipps has plotted Darwin's 'religious odyssey'. On the question of theodicy, he comments, 'Darwin asked the perennial question: How can one believe in a just and merciful Omnipotence who allows personal tragedy to the undeserving? Had he studied Job, he might have gained insight into relating unmerited suffering to theology and natural selection.'[20] One thing can be asserted strongly: Darwin never wholly renounced his faith. Towards the end of his life he replied to the atheist John Fordyce who asked if belief in evolution and God was compatible, that 'It seems to me absurd to doubt that a man may be an ardent Theist

---

object which we are capable of conceiving, the production of the higher animals, directly follows. There is grandeur in this view of life with its several powers, having been originally breathed by the Creator into a few forms or into one; and that, whilst this planet has gone cycling on according to the fixed law of gravity, from so simple a beginning endless forms most beautiful and most wonderful have been, and are being evolved.'

19. J. R. Moore, *The Darwin Legend* (London: Hodder & Stoughton, 1994); idem, 'Telling Tales. Evangelicals and the Darwin Legend', in D. N. Livingstone, D. G. Hart and M. A. Noll (eds.), *Evangelicals and Science in Historical Perspective* (New York: Oxford University Press, 1999), pp. 220–233.

20. William Phipps, *Darwin's Religious Odyssey* (Harrisburg: Trinity International, 2002), p. 185.

and an evolutionist . . . as to my own views . . . in my most extreme
fluctuations I have never been an atheist in the sense of denying
the existence of a God'. One of his last letters was to Professor
William Graham, Professor of Political Economy in Belfast, in
which he declared 'my inward conviction [is] that the Universe is
not the result of chance'. However, the issue for us is not Darwin's
own religious views, but the impact of his ideas on those who have
received them over the last 150 years.[21] To quote Phipps again,
'Darwin's account of evolution has probably changed our outlook
on human and divine existence more than any other theory in
the history of human thought. Accounts of presumed miraculous
interventions by an omnipotent God have become a liability rather
than an asset to theology'.[22]

---

21. Letter 12041, 7 May 1879; letter 13230, 3 July 1881. The emphasis in
    this essay is on Darwin's *science*. 'Darwinism' has been extrapolated into
    a range of social, economic, political and other fields which are distant
    and almost entirely unrelated to biological evolution and the evolution-
    ary mechanisms put forward by Darwin. Karl Giberson comments. 'The
    energy [for the many challenges to evolution] did not come from wide-
    spread concern that evolution was incompatible with the Bible, although
    that was certainly a background issue. The energy came from the belief
    that evolution was the foundation of evil social agendas. In this sense the
    anti-evolutionary campaign was more like the war on drugs than a war of
    ideas' (*Saving Darwin* [New York: HarperCollins, 2008], p. 118). See also
    n. 37.
22. Phipps, *Darwin's Religious Odyssey*, n. 20, p. 198. John Polkinghorne
    encapsulates this: 'In an earlier age, miracles would have been one of the
    strongest weapons in the armoury of apologetic. A man who did such
    things must at the very least have the power of God with him. Jesus
    himself is represented as using this argument when he said "If it is by the
    finger of God that I cast out demons, then the kingdom of God has come
    upon you" (Lk 11: 20). For us today, by one of those twists that make
    up intellectual history, miracles are rather an embarrassment. We are so
    impressed by the regularity of the world that any story which is full of
    strange happenings acquires an air of fairy tale and invention' (*The Way the
    World Is* [London: SPCK, 1983], p. 54).

Evolution and Emma

Darwin's view of the natural world began to change through his observations that animal species replaced each other along the length of South America and that fossils often resembled – but differed in details from – similar living forms. Notwithstanding he retained a 'traditional' belief in a world more or less unaltered from its creation until after the *Beagle* voyage. The trigger that finally shifted his views seems to have been a conversation in March 1837 with John Gould, the ornithologist at the London Zoo, to whom Darwin had entrusted the bird specimens he had collected. Gould's finding that the finches on the Galapagos were an entirely new group wholly confined to those islands, forced him to rethink his earlier assumption of a static world.[23] He made a note for himself, 'the Zoology of Archipelagoes will be well worth examining, for such facts would undermine the stability of species'.

By 1842, Darwin was sufficiently sure of his new understanding of biological change to describe it in a brief thirty-five-page 'sketch'; he expanded this into a 200-page 'Essay' in 1844. The latter formed the basis of the *Origin of Species*, published in 1859. His starting point was a Paleyian belief that the Creator creates by laws.[24] It involved a very simple mechanism, based on three facts and two deductions. He began with the observation that virtually all species have a large potential for increase in number (think of the number of acorns produced by an oak tree or the masses of frog spawn laid by every female frog), but (second observation) numbers remain roughly constant. The inference from this is that there must be a *struggle for existence*, with only a small proportion of young surviving. The existence of such a struggle is essentially an ecological deduction and one well understood in Darwin's time. It forced itself on Darwin's awareness when in 1838 he read 'for amusement', Thomas Malthus's *Essay on the Principles of Population*,

23. F. Sulloway, 'Darwin's conversion: the *Beagle* voyage and its aftermath', *Journal of the History of Biology* 15 (1982), pp. 325–396.

24. D. Ospovat, *The Development of Darwin's Theory* (Cambridge: Cambridge University Press, 1979). See also n. 18 above.

which set out the spectre of the human population outstripping its food supply with the weak and improvident succumbing in the resulting struggle for resources. Darwin's genius was in linking a third fact – heritable variation – to the ever-prevalent struggle for existence.[25] If only a small proportion of a population survives the struggle, the likelihood is that it will include a high proportion of those with any trait which gives them some sort of advantage. Over the generations, those carrying the trait will increase in frequency at the expense of those lacking the trait. There would be a genetic change in the population, amounting to *natural selection* for the trait in question.

Darwin used the way that human selection had changed domesticated breeds of animals as a model of the processes happening in nature. His contemporary, Herbert Spencer, a railway engineer turned philosopher, coined the phrase 'survival of the fittest' to describe the process.[26] This has been a source of much

---

25. In his *Autobiography*, Darwin wrote: 'At that time I overlooked one problem of great importance ... the tendency in organic beings descended from the same stock to diverge in character as they became modified. That they diverged greatly is obvious from the manner in which species of all kinds can be classed under genera, genera under families, families under sub-orders, and so forth; and I can remember the very spot in the road, whilst in my carriage, when to my joy the solution came to me; and this was long after I had come to Down [1842]. The solution, as I believe, is that the modified offspring of all dominant and increasing forms tend to become adapted to many and highly diversified places in the economy of nature' (Barlow, *Autobiography*, n. 15, pp. 120–121).

26. Spencer's influence on evolutionary debates has been almost entirely malign. Darwin proposed a theory of organic change; Spencer a metaphysic based on change (J. R. Durant (ed.), *Darwinism and Divinity* [Oxford: Blackwell, 1985]). Spencer extrapolated the idea of natural selection to human social structures ('social Darwinism'), encouraging industrialists (particularly in the US) to claim that inefficiency and failure were part of a 'natural' (and hence God-given) struggle for existence. Spencer's ideas have certainly encouraged anti-evolutionism in the US, expressed in many publications from religious organizations and in the declared aim of the

confusion and repeated accusations that natural selection is tautologous. This is wrong: 'fitness' in its biological sense refers to reproductive success, not health or physical prowess. The 'fittest' are those who raise most offspring – which properly describes natural selection.

The *Origin of Species* was published on 24 November 1859, price 15 shillings (£0.75). Twelve hundred copies were printed and sold out straightaway; a reprint was immediately needed. Darwin intended it merely as 'an abstract' of an intended Big Book on evolution, which he had begun writing three years earlier. His plans for the 'Big Book' were thrown awry when in June 1858 he received a letter from Alfred Russel Wallace – written when he was recovering from fever on the Indonesian island of Ternate in the Moluccas (or Malukus) – asking him to comment on a manuscript setting out a possible mechanism for evolutionary change. Wallace's proposals were almost identical with Darwin's. Darwin felt he was morally obliged to pass on Wallace's paper for publication, but he was persuaded by his friends Charles Lyell (the leading geologist of the time) and Joseph Hooker (soon to follow his father as Director of the Royal Botanic Gardens at Kew) to allow parts of his 1844 'Essay' to be read at a meeting of the Linnean Society in 1858 at the same time as Wallace's communication. And it was this that forced him to write the book we know as the *Origin* in a hurry.

The reason for the delay in publishing between 1844 and 1858 has been subject to much speculation. Clearly Darwin wanted to accumulate as much evidence as possible for his theory. He was aware of some of the implications of his ideas and the opposition that they would attract. He was alarmed by the explosion in 1844 provoked by the publication of the *Vestiges of the Natural History of Creation* by Robert Chambers.[27] Chambers wrote that when there is a choice between special creation and the operation of

---

Institute for Creation Research to reverse 'the harmful consequences of evolutionary thinking on families and society (abortion, promiscuity, drug abuse, homosexuality, and many others)'.

27. London: John Churchill.

general laws instituted by the Creator, 'I would say that the latter
is generally preferable as it implies a far grander view of the divine
power than the other.' Since there was nothing in the inorganic
world 'which may not be accounted for by the agency of the ordinary forces of nature', why not consider 'the possibility of plants
and animals having likewise been produced in a natural way'. The
Vestiges was effectively a tract against the Deism of William Paley's
version of natural theology.[28] It was an immediate best-seller. In
the ten years following its publication, it sold more copies than
did the *Origin* fifteen years later. But it was full of errors. For
Darwin, 'the writing and arrangement are certainly admirable, but
the geology strikes me as bad & his zoology far worse'. Others
roundly condemned the book. Adam Sedgwick lambasted it in an
eighty-five-page diatribe in the *Edinburgh Review*; he called it 'a foul
book [in which] gross credulity and rank infidelity join in unlaw-
ful marriage'.[29] He wrote to his colleague Charles Lyell, 'If the
book be true, the labours of sober induction are in vain; religion
is a lie; human law is a mass of folly and a base injustice; morality is moonshine; our labours for the black people of Africa were
works of madmen; and man and woman are only better beasts.' Its
importance is the debate it stirred. Despite his misgivings about it,
Darwin welcomed the book on the grounds that 'it has done excel-
lent service in calling in this country attention to the subject and in
removing prejudices'.

But the criticisms of the *Vestiges* alarmed him.[30] Its author was

---

28. J. A. Secord, *Victorian Sensation* (Chicago: University of Chicago Press,
    2000).

29. *Edinburgh Review*, July 1845. Sedgwick confessed that 'reviewing was
    more like writing a sermon than composing a scientific paper' (ibid, n. 28,
    p. 246).

30. Note should also be taken of *Omphalos. An Attempt to Untie the Geological
    Knot*, a 378-page plea from Philip Gosse, a distinguished naturalist
    and friend of Darwin, published in 1857 just as Darwin was getting
    down to writing his 'Big Book'. Gosse desperately wanted to preserve
    a literal interpretation for Genesis 1 and to destroy any evidence for
    evolution. He argued that God might have created the world 'as if' it

widely attacked as a wild speculator, not to be taken seriously. Darwin's knowledge of the natural world was extensive, but it was not deep. Soon after the *Vestiges* appeared, Hooker commented in a letter to Darwin (September 1845) (*a propos* a book on the nature of species by a French botanist, Frédéric Gérard, whom Hooker disparaged because he was 'neither a specific naturalist, nor a collector, not a traveller . . . and therefore a distorter of facts'), that to be qualified to speculate about the nature of species, 'one must have handled hundreds of species with a view to distinguishing them & that over a great part – or brought from many parts – of the globe. I am not inclined to take much for granted from any one who treats the subject in his way and who does not know what it is to be a specific Naturalist himself'. Hooker seemed to assume that Darwin fulfilled these requirements, but Darwin was alarmed. He responded to Hooker, 'No one has the right to examine the question of species who has not minutely examined many'. He began a study of the barnacles he had collected on the *Beagle* cruise. This extended into a detailed investigation of barnacles worldwide and occupied him from 1846 to 1854, culminating in four massive monographs, two on living barnacles and two on fossil forms, an achievement which remains as a definitive treatment of the group.[31] The Royal Society gave him a Royal Medal for the work. But Darwin's barnacle explorations were more than a self-justifying exercise: they opened his eyes to variation within species and the apparent relationships of different families. When

---

was ancient. The difficulty was that this implied that God was devious. The book was widely ridiculed. The *Westminster Review* denounced it as 'too monstrous for belief'; the *Natural History Review* concluded that it was 'idle speculations, fit only to please a philosopher in his hours of relaxation, but hardly worthy of the serious attentions of any earnest man, whether scientific or not'. It had little impact and most copies of the book were pulped (A. Thwaite, *Glimpses of the Wonderful. The Life of Philip Henry Gosse* [London: Faber, 2002]). Notwithstanding, Gosse's proposal remains the only logical (albeit unfaithful to reality) alternative to evolution.

31. R. Stott, *Darwin and the Barnacle* (London: Faber & Faber, 2003).

he returned to his 'transformism' he was much more aware of biological complications in the real world than previously.[32]

A third and certainly a major reason for Darwin's procrastina-
tion about evolutionary publication, was consideration for his
wife's views. Emma was a quiet but devout Anglican. A month
before their marriage, she had written to Charles,

> I thank you from my heart for your openness with me. My reason tells
> me that honest and conscientious doubts cannot be a sin, but I feel it
> could be a painful void between us. I thank you from my heart for your
> openness with me & I should dread the feeling that you were concealing
> your opinions from the fear of giving me pain. It is perhaps foolish of
> me to say this much but my own dear Charley we now do belong to each
> other & I cannot help being open with you. Will you do me a favour?
> yes I am sure you will, it is to read our Saviours farewell discourse to his
> disciples which begins at the end of the 13th Chap of John. It is so full
> of love to them & devotion & every beautiful feeling. It is the part of
> the New Testament I love best. This is a whim of mine it would give me
> great pleasure.

Shortly after their wedding Emma wrote again (February 1839),

> May not the habit in scientific pursuits of believing nothing till it is
> proved, influence your mind too much in other things which cannot
> be proved in the same way, & which if true are likely to be above our
> comprehension. I should say also that there is a danger in giving up
> revelation which does not exist on the other side. Every thing that
> concerns you concerns me & I should be most unhappy if I thought we
> did not belong to each other forever.

Whatever the reason, it is proper to date the beginning of
the modern era in biology to a meeting of the Linnean Society
in Burlington House on Piccadilly, London on 1 July 1858.

---

32. R. Bellon, 'Joseph Hooker Takes a "Fixed Post": Transmutation and the
    "Present Unsatisfactory State of Systematic Botany", 1844–1860', *Journal
    of the History of Biology* 39 (2006), pp. 1–39.

Surprisingly in historical hindsight, the meeting attracted little attention. A few months later, the Linnean President noted, 'The year that has passed has not been marked by any of those striking discoveries which revolutionise the department of science on which they bear.' How gloriously wrong he was only became apparent following the appearance of the *Origin* seventeen months later. Emotions flared at the time. But not all reactions were antagonistic. One of the first responses to Darwin came in a letter from Charles Kingsley, at the time Rector of Eversley in Hampshire but soon to become Regius Professor of Modern History at Cambridge. Kingsley wrote, 'I find it just as noble a conception of Deity to believe that He created primal forms capable of self development . . . as to believe that He required a fresh act of intervention to supply the *lacunas* which He himself had made.'

Spread of Darwinism

Darwin's arguments were quickly accepted, contrary to repeated assertions that they were highly contentious and 'only a theory'. Frederick Temple, Bishop of Exeter and soon to become Archbishop of Canterbury gave them an *imprimatur* in his Bampton Lectures published in 1885, '[God] did not make the things, we may say; but He made them make themselves'.[33] Ironically Darwin's ideas were assimilated more readily by conservative theologians than by liberals, apparently because of the formers' stronger doctrine of providence.[34] Many of the authors of the 'Fundamentals', the series of booklets produced between 1910 and 1915 to expound the 'fundamental beliefs' of Protestant theology as defined by the General Assembly of the American Presbyterian Church, were sympathetic to evolution. Princeton theologian

33. F. Temple, *The Relations Between Religion and Science* (London: Macmillan, 1885), p. 115.

34. D. N. Livingstone, *Darwin's Forgotten Defenders. The Encounter Between Evangelical Theology and Evolutionary Thought* (Grand Rapids: Eerdmans, 1987).

B. B. Warfield, a passionate advocate of the inerrancy of the Bible, stated, 'I do not think that there is any general statement in the Bible . . . that need be opposed to evolution . . .'[35] He believed that evolution could provide a tenable 'theory of the method of divine providence in the creation of mankind'.[36]

The infamous debate between the Bishop of Oxford and Thomas Huxley at the 1860 meeting of the British Association for the Advancement of Science was not really about evolution versus creation or even science versus religion. On the Bishop's side it was about the danger of legitimizing change in an age when he believed it was having dangerous social and theological effects; Huxley's aim was the secularization of society – to establish the legitimacy of science against what he regarded as the improper influence of church leaders.[37] It was reported that Wilberforce

35. B. B. Warfield, *Evolution or Development* (1888). Cited by M. A. Noll and
    D. N. Livingstone (eds.), *B. B. Warfield. Evolution, Science and Scripture*
    (Grand Rapids: Baker, 2000), p. 130.
36. B. B. Warfield, 'Calvin's Doctrine of the Creation', *Princeton Theological
    Review* 13 (1915), pp. 190–255, p. 209. Warfield cannot be dismissed
    as uniquely idiosyncratic in accepting evolutionary ideas. Noll and
    Livingstone quote James Packer as being unable to see anything in the
    early chapters of Genesis that 'bears on the biological theory of evolu-
    tion one way or the other . . . I recall that B. B. Warfield was a theistic
    evolutionist. If on this count I am not an evangelical, then neither was he'
    (Noll and Livingstone, *Warfield*, n. 33, p. 38). Gordon Wenham writes,
    'Neither exact sequence nor the mechanisms that God used in creation is
    of great interest in Genesis . . . A wide variety of scientific hypotheses are
    compatible with its [Gen 1–3] theological affirmations. What is incompat-
    ible with Genesis is an atheistic interpretation of the origins of life' (M. W.
    Poole and G. J. Wenham, *Creation or Evolution – a False Antithesis?* [Oxford:
    Latimer Studies Nos. 23/24, 1987], p. 31–32.
37. The other well-known evolution-creation contest – the 1926 Scopes
    'Monkey Trial' – in Dayton, Tennessee, was also really about other issues:
    the self-promotion of a small town, the freedom of expression under
    the American constitution, the agenda of a populist politician (William
    Jennings Bryan), and the ambitions of the American Civil Liberties Union

went away happy that he had given Huxley a bloody nose, while
Joseph Hooker (who spoke after Huxley) told Darwin that Huxley
had been largely inaudible. As far as the audience was concerned,
many scored it as an entertaining draw.[38] The tragedy has been a
legacy of inevitable conflict between science and faith, encouraged by Huxley himself and fuelled by two much-read manifestos
by John William Draper (*History of the Conflict between Religion and
Science*, 1875) and Andrew Dickson White (*A History of the Warfare of
Science with Theology in Christendom*, 1886).[39]

It is worth noting that Darwin (and Wallace) was concerned with
a possible *mechanism* for evolutionary change, not with the actual
existence of change. The mechanism (often called 'Darwinism') is
patently open to test and therefore possible of disproof, contrary
to the claim often made by modern anti-evolutionists that it is
dogma rather than science. The widely-quoted criticism (albeit
later retracted) by Karl Popper that 'Darwinism is not a testable
scientific theory but a metaphysical research programme' was
based on his rejection of all 'historical' sciences (because they

---

for a test case (E. J. Larson, *Summer for the Gods. The Scopes Trial and America's
Continuing Debate over Science and Religion* [Cambridge, MA: Harvard
University Press, 1997]; Giberson, *Saving Darwin*, see n. 21). Like the
Wilberforce-Huxley debate and helped by a Broadway play later filmed
as *Inherit the Wind*, it has become a formidable myth about the triumph of
science over prejudice.

38. J. H. Brooke, 'The Wilberforce-Huxley Debate: Why Did It Happen?',
Science and Christian Belief 13 (2001), pp. 127–141.

39. Colin Russell comments: 'Today the historical views of Draper and White
are totally unacceptable, not merely because of many factual aberrations,
but much more because they represent a long demolished tradition of
positivist, Whiggish historiography . . . Draper . . . was gripped by the fear
of the power wielded by the Roman Catholic church. White was President
of Cornell, the first non-sectarian university in the USA. His enemies had
been those advocates of sectarian theology to whom the very existence
of Cornell was a tangible threat . . . His book was directed not so much
against religion as against dogmatic theology' ('The Conflict Metaphor
and Its Social Origins', *Science and Christian Belief* 1 [1989], pp. 3–26, p. 6).

were non-falsifiable), plus a misunderstanding of the Darwinian mechanism.[40]

Although Charles Darwin can properly be said to have introduced a revolution in thought and understanding, it would be wrong to assume that the idea of evolution emerged suddenly in 1858. Darwin himself acknowledged a swarm of scholars who had preceded him in believing that species were subject to change into new species (*transformism* in the language of the time). Probably his best known antecedent is Jean-Baptiste Lamarck, a Frenchman who worked in the Natural History Museum in Paris from 1788 until his death in 1829. Lamarck believed that there was a progressive increase in perfection from the simplest organisms to its peak in humankind; he argued that over a long period of time, one species would become transformed into another 'higher' one. This got over the problem of species extinction, which seemed to contradict the notion of a perfect world created by God and which was becoming increasingly contentious in the late eighteenth century as it became clear that organisms found as fossils were not still surviving in a yet undiscovered El Dorado.

During the same period, geologists were massively extending the history of the Earth from the assumption derived from the biblical genealogies that creation took place around six thousand years ago.[41] In 1788 James Hutton, the 'father of modern geology' argued in his *Theory of the Earth* that the world was almost infinitely old. It is worth emphasizing that this change in understanding was entirely a result of observations of the real world. It caused Bible expositors to look again at their interpretation of Genesis, but the emergence of the science of geology should not be taken as an intended challenge to the Scriptures.[42] The realiza-

---

40. Popper made his retraction in a letter to the *New Scientist* 87 (1980), p. 611. For a full account of this episode, see D. N. Stamos, 'Popper, Falsifiability and Evolutionary Biology', *Biology and Philosophy* 11 (1996), pp. 161–191.

41. C. L. E. Lewis and S. J. Knell (eds.), *The Age of the Earth: from 4004 BC to AD 2002* (London: Geological Society Special Publication No. 190, 2001).

42. C. C. Gillispie, *Genesis and Geology* (Cambridge, MA: Harvard University Press, 1951); D. A. Young, *Christianity and the Age of the Earth* (Grand

tion of a long Earth history allowed time for the procession of change assumed by Lamarck, but it was the Achilles heel of traditional natural theology. A creator could presumably design an organism perfectly adapted to a particular environment, but this perfection would disappear if the environment was not constant. Adjusting to changes in climate, to the physical structure of the Earth's surface, or to predators and competitors is possible only if organisms can adapt. All this produced considerable theological ferment in the first half of the nineteenth century which is not relevant here.[43] Suffice it to say that by 1859, the majority of Bible expositors accepted a non-literal interpretation of the early chapters of Genesis.[44]

Darwin was well aware that his ideas would be criticized, and two chapters in the *Origin* were devoted to 'difficulties' and 'objections' to his theory. Fisher[45] commented that 'the cogency and wealth of illustrations with which Darwin was able to deal with these cases was, perhaps the largest factor in persuading biologists of the truth of his views'. The most persistent criticism has been that natural selection is merely a negative influence, removing inefficiency but incapable of producing novelty or seemingly perfect adaptations like a mammalian eye or the pattern of a butterfly's wing. Darwin pointed out that the function of a trait may change with time; it is wrong to speculate about the history of a particular organ as if it has always had the same role for its possessors. These arguments have been strengthened and

Rapids: Zondervan, 1982); R. L. Stiling, 'Scriptural Geology in America', in Livingstone, Hart and Noll (eds.), *Evangelicals and Science*, pp. 177–192.

43. Gillispie, *Genesis and Geology*, n. 42; J. R. Moore, 'Geologists and Interpreters of Genesis in the Nineteenth Century', in D. C. Lindberg and R. L. Numbers (eds.), *God and Nature* (Berkeley: University of California Press, 1986), pp. 322–350.

44. M. B. Roberts, 'Darwin's Doubts About Design – The Darwin-Gray Correspondence of 1860', *Science and Christian Belief* 9 (1997), pp. 113–127.

45. R. A. Fisher, 'Retrospect of the Criticisms of the Theory of Natural Selection', in J. Huxley, A. C. Hardy and E. B. Ford (eds.), *Evolution as a Process* (London: Allen & Unwin, 1954), p. 89.

the credibility of natural selection has grown enormously since genome mapping became a reality, revealing a remarkable and previously unsuspected developmental flexibility. For example, the crystalline proteins which make up the eye lens have been repeatedly and independently 'redeployed' since their origin as stress-related proteins in microorganisms. Conway Morris has identified '20 or even more independent lines of differentiation [towards eye perfection], including at least 15 cases of independent attainments of photoreceptors with a distinct lens'. Many genes are duplicated in putative lineages, allowing new functions to develop because of the flexibility produced by the introduction of such 'spare genes'.[46]

A common criticism of natural selection is that it is dependent on randomly occurring mutation. This is a frequent accusation of 'creationists', but extends much wider than the beliefs of anti-evolutionists. It was the basis of Jacques Monod's nihilistic *Chance and Necessity*.[47] However it is misplaced. The Darwinian process does not depend on chance: adaptation results from the selection of advantageous variants, and this is a deterministic process. The confusion arises because the origin of inherited variation is random, depending on mutation or, much more significantly in sexual organisms, on the phenotypic expression of new variants

46. S. Conway Morris, *Life's Solution. Inevitable Humans in a Lonely Universe* (Cambridge: Cambridge University Press, 2003). The impact of genome analysis on establishing relationship and descent is regularly misunderstood by critics of Darwinism. For example, Ranald Macaulay (*Evangelicals Now*, November 2008) suggests that it is merely a restatement of the 'morphology principle' ('shared structures in the animal kingdom that in themselves prove nothing'). A comprehensive refutation of such an assumption has been provided by Graeme Finlay ('Evolution as Created History', *Science and Christian Belief* 20 [2008], pp. 67–89). A readable overview of current understanding is given by Sean Carroll, *The Making of the Fittest. DNA and the Ultimate Forensic Record of Evolution* (New York: W. W. Norton, 2008).

47. London: Collins, 1971. See the response by W. H. Thorpe, *Purpose in a World of Chance* (Oxford: Oxford University Press, 1978).

through recombination. Whilst it is true that adaptation relates to survival and the possibility of gene transmission rather than long-term purpose, it is wrong to claim that 'Darwinian evolution' is an entirely fortuitous process. Indeed Simon Conway Morris has shown that the range of viable options for any trait is so limited that it may lead to the appearance of purposive progress.[48] Natural selection is the only mechanism (apart from divine intervention) which fits organisms to their environment.

We can identify four major periods of debate about evolution-ary science:

- in the decades immediately following the publication of the *Origin*;
- Mendelian biometrician disputes around 1900 and the search for 'progress', particularly by liberal theologians and social scientists;
- a split between geneticists and palaeontologists, effectively resolved by the neo-Darwinian synthesis;
- neutralism and selectionism in the 1970s.

A problem that troubled Darwin himself was that variation is apparently lost in every mating, because offspring are generally speaking intermediate between their parents. This was resolved by the discovery of particulate inheritance – the recognition that inherited elements (genes) are transmitted unchanged between generations. The appearance of blending is because the expression of every gene is modified by other genes. This was the essence of Gregor Mendel's work, published in 1865 but only realized as significant when it was 'rediscovered' in 1900. But in solving one problem, it raised another for the Darwinians: the genes studied by the early geneticists (or Mendelians, as they were called) were almost all deleterious to their carriers, had large effects, and were inherited as recessives – all properties which seemed counter to

48. Conway Morris, *Life's Solution*, n. 46; R. J. Berry, 'Nothing in Biology Makes Sense Except in the Light of Evolution', *Science and Christian Belief* 18 (2006), pp. 23–29.

the progressive gradualism expected under Darwinism. A rift appeared between the biometricians studying the evidence of evolution in living or fossil populations and the geneticists who were unquestionably uncovering the physical basis of heredity.[49]

This impasse persisted and widened through the first decades of the twentieth century. There were no real doubts that large-scale evolution had occurred, but it did not seem to have been driven by natural selection. Vernon Kellogg spoke of 'the death-bed of Darwinism' in his introduction to a book written for the jubilee of the *Origin* in 1908. He wrote, 'Darwinism as the all-sufficient or even the most important causo-mechanical factor in species-forming and hence as the sufficient explanation of descent, is discredited and cast down.'[50] Into this apparent void, an extravagance of other evolutionary theories poured: Berg's *Nomogenesis*, Willis's *Age and Area*, Smut's *Holism*, Driesch's entelechy, Osborn's aristogenesis and orthogenesis. Invention was rife. A common feature was some form of inner progressionist urge or *élan vital*. Unfortunately three standard and still-read histories of biology (by Nordenskiöld, Rádl and Singer) were written during this time, perpetuating the idea that evolutionary theory is an illogical mess and that Darwinism is completely eclipsed.

The scientific confusion spread into theology. The idea that evolution was driven by some sort of purpose was influentially espoused by some distinguished scientists – the zoologist Ray Lankester and the physiologist J. S. Haldane, the psychologists Lloyd Morgan, William McDougall and E. S. Russell, physicists like Oliver Lodge, and the cosmologists A. S. Eddington and James Jeans; as well as by popularizers like Arthur Thomson and politicians such as Arthur Balfour. Not surprisingly with such apparently informed authorities, these ideas were seized upon by churchmen, prominent among them being Charles Gore, and somewhat later W. R. Inge, Hensley Henson, Charles Raven and E. W. Barnes.

---

49. W. B. Provine, *The Origin of Theoretical Population Genetics* (Chicago: Chicago University Press, 1971).

50. V. L. Kellogg, *Darwinism Today* (London: George Bell & Sons, 1907), p. 374.

This crossover of evolutionary idealism from science to theology has been elegantly chronicled by Peter Bowler.[51] It eventually died through its perceived ineffectiveness rather than conscious rejection. 'The Modernists saw themselves marginalized not by the new science, of which many remained unaware, but by changing values within the churches, which brought back a sense of human sinfulness and alienation from God incompatible with the idea of progress.'[52] One can have some sympathy with the theologians. It took the scientists a long time to reach an evolutionary synthesis, but this does not excuse uncritical use of inadequate science.

The neo-Darwinian synthesis

The irrelevance of the frenzy of evolutionary speculating was exposed by a series of theoretical analyses in the 1920s, beginning with two difficult and largely non-understood papers by R. A. Fisher, in which he showed that continuous variation could arise through the cumulative effect of many genes, each with a small effect, and that dominance was the result of interaction between genes rather than an intrinsic property of a gene by itself.[53] He argued that the dominance or recessivity of any character is the consequence of repeated mutation during evolutionary time, with modification of its effect by other genes – towards greater expression if its effects were beneficial to its carrier or lesser if it had deleterious effects (i.e. its expression will be modified towards dominance or recessivity respectively), thus removing the difficulties raised by the early Mendelians.

Fisher's analyses were complemented by J. B. S. Haldane in

51. P. J. Bowler, *Reconciling Science and Religion* (Chicago: Chicago University Press, 2001).

52. Ibid., n. 51, p. 417.

53. 'The Correlation Between Relatives on the Supposition of Mendelian Inheritance', *Transactions of the Royal Society of Edinburgh* 52 (1918), pp. 399–433; 'On the Dominance Ratio', *Proceedings of the Royal Society of Edinburgh* 42 (1922), pp. 321–341.

Britain and Sewall Wright in the United States, and summarized in a series of major works.[54] They were supported by studies of inherited variation in natural populations by E. B. Ford (1931) in Britain and Theodosius Dobzhansky (1937) in the US.[55] Their conclusions, together with results from many other sources, were brought together by Julian Huxley in a book *Evolution: The Modern Synthesis* (1942), which provided the eponymous name to the incorporation of Mendelian genetics into the insights of Darwin, and the final reconciliation of the earlier evolutionary debates.[56]

The Mendelian or neo-Darwinian synthesis of the 1940s has proved to be a robust understanding of evolutionary processes as well as a justification of Darwin's original theory.[57] Its most serious challenge came in the 1960s when biochemical techniques of protein analysis were applied to variation in natural populations and unexpectedly large amounts of inherited variation discovered – between one in four and one in twenty genes tended to be represented by slightly different forms (*alleles*) on the chromosomes an individual receives from the two parents. Conventional understanding was that such high levels of variation would lead to an unsupportable 'genetic load' because the less advantageous allele would reduce the reproductive potential of its carrier. The simplest escape from this dilemma was to assume that such biochemical variants had no effect on their bearer (i.e. that they were 'neutral' and thus not subject to selection). This argument seemed to be

---

54. R. A. Fisher, *The Genetical Theory of Natural Selection* (Oxford: Clarendon Press, 1930); S. Wright, 'Evolution in Mendelian Populations', *Genetics* 16 (1931), pp. 97–159; J. B. S. Haldane, *The Causes of Evolution* (London: Longmans, 1932).

55. E. B. Ford, *Mendelism and Evolution* (London: Methuen, 1931); Th. Dobzhansky, *Genetics and the Origin of Species* (New York: Columbia University Press, 1937).

56. London: Allen & Unwin.

57. E. Mayr and W. B. Provine (eds.), *The Evolutionary Synthesis* (Cambridge, MA: Harvard University Press, 1980); R. J. Berry, *Neo-Darwinism* (London: Edward Arnold, 1982).

supported by apparently regular rates of accumulation of new variants (mutations), to the extent that a 'molecular (or protein) clock' could be calibrated on the basis of the number of gene differences between two lineages.

However it soon appeared that the protein clock did not keep good time. Different proteins could change at rates differing by two orders of magnitude while the same protein may change faster (or slower) in different groups. These are effects that would be expected if the proteins were subject to selection rather than a physically determined mutation rate. The falsifying of extreme neutralist assumptions led to attention being refocused on environmental (or ecological) factors in evolution. For example, it is improper to speak of *the* selective effect of an inherited character. Selection varies in both time and space. It may be density- or frequency-dependent or independent. In the well-known example of moths being selectively predated by birds, the chance of being eaten (i.e. the intensity of selection) varies with the amount and history of atmospheric pollution. Places where black moths had a high survival rate have changed as pollution has declined following clean air legislation, and the survival rate of black moths has declined in proportion.

A positive outcome of the neutralism debates has been to rescue evolutionary studies from the danger of overdependence on theoretical models and lead them back to an observation and experimental basis – which is where Darwin and Wallace began.[58]

Only an ape?

However the biggest theological challenges for Darwinian ideas concern human evolution. Anxious to minimize controversy, Darwin steered clear of human evolution in the *Origin*. He included only one mention of the subject, 'I see open fields for far more

---

58. R. J. Berry, 'Ecology: Where Genes and Geography Meet', *Journal of Animal Ecology* 58 (1989), pp. 733–759; R. J. Berry, T. J. S. Crawford and G. M. Hewitt (eds.), *Genes in Ecology* (Oxford: Blackwell Scientific, 1992).

important researches . . . Much light will be thrown on the origin of man and his history.'[59] However, he could not ignore the topic altogether, and returned to it fourteen years later with the *Descent of Man.* He 'warned friends that it would seem "very wicked"; Churchmen would think him "an outcast & a reprobate"; he expected "universal disapprobation, if not execution" – meaning, he told a critic, that the book would "quite kill me in your good estimation".'[60]

Darwin knew almost nothing about human fossils. The first Neanderthal fossils were only found in 1858. But since that time, many putative hominoid and hominid fossils have been discovered, to the extent that it is fair to claim that *Homo* has a better fossil record than almost any other genus. Unfortunately its credibility has been marred in popular understanding by over-imaginative reconstruction of particular finds, notably the Piltdown debacle, but also by many fanciful attempts to portray human ancestors as either hulking brutes or mere variants of modern individuals.[61] The image of human fossil history for many is probably the much-reproduced frontispiece of T. H. Huxley's *Man's Place in Nature* (1863),[62] showing a parade of modern skeletons from a gibbon, through a series of stooping apes, to an upright man ('A grim and grotesque procession' as Darwin's critic, the eighth Duke of Argyll, called it). Notwithstanding and recognizing many uncertainties, there is now general agreement among specialists that *Homo* originated from an *Australopithecus* stock in Africa, with the first fossils classified in the genus *Homo* occurring between 2.0

---

59. In 1857, Darwin wrote to Wallace about his planned book on 'transmutation': 'You ask whether I shall discuss "man". I think I shall avoid the whole subject, as so surrounded with prejudices; though I fully admit it is the highest and most interesting problem for the naturalist.'

60. J. R. Moore and A. Desmond, in the Introduction to *The Descent of Man* (London: Penguin Classics, 2004), p. xv.

61. A good account of this over-enthusiasm is given by P. J. Bowler, *Theories of Human Evolution: A Century of Debates 1844–1944* (Oxford: Basil Blackwell, 1986).

62. London: Williams & Norgate.

and 1.6 million years ago; they are named *Homo habilis*. About 1.8 million years ago, a new form of *Homo* appeared in eastern Africa, *H. erectus*. It persisted in Africa for more than a million years, but also spread out of Africa into Asia.[63] It had a brain size (or more strictly, cranial volume) of 800–900 ml, about a third greater than *H. habilis*, and a less projecting face. Four hundred thousand years ago, the earliest fossils regarded as *H. sapiens* (brain size *c.* 1,100–1,300 ml) occur. They have been found in Africa, Europe and China. 'Neanderthal man' appeared *c.* 200,000 years ago in Europe and south-west Asia. It is now regarded as at least sub-specifically different from *H. sapiens*, and coexisted with the latter until disappearing 30,000 to 40,000 years ago.[64]

Developments in molecular biology have strengthened the recognition of our genetic closeness to the other primates. An earlier calculation that humans and chimps share 98.4% of their genes has been refined now that both genomes have been sequenced; nevertheless there is a clear identity between more than 95% of the genes in the two species.[65] Notwithstanding, our DNA differences from the chimpanzees amount to around 10,000 nucleotide changes, most of them in so-called 'junk DNA' which regulates the activity of protein-coding sequences. We have one less pair of chromosomes than all other apes (23 pairs instead of 24), but the difference is the simple result of end-to-end fusion between two separate elements of the ape chromosome set.

There is no evidence that there are many novel genes in the human genome. Around 8% of the human genome apparently consists of retroviral inserts influencing gene regulation in

63. C. Finlayson, 'Biogeography and Evolution of the Genus *Homo*', *Trends in Ecology and Evolution* 20 (2005), pp. 457–463.

64. C. Stringer, 'Modern Human Origins – Progress and Prospects', *Philosophical Transactions of the Royal Society of London* B 357 (2002), pp. 563–579; J. H. Relethford, 'Genetic Evidence and the Modern Human Origins Debate', *Heredity* 100 (2008), pp. 555–563.

65. R. J. Britten, 'Divergence Between Samples of Chimpanzee and Human DNA Sequences is 5%, Counting Indels', *Proceedings of the National Academy of Sciences of the USA* 99 (2002), pp. 13633–13635.

significant ways. There does not seem to be evidence of positive selection between chimps and humans for genes concerned
with brain development or function as a whole. One of the most
intriguing results so far from comparative molecular genetics is
that since the human and chimpanzee lines separated around six
million years ago, a third more chimpanzee genes show signs of
selection than do human ones. Put another way, this implies that
chimpanzees are more specialized than humans; we are general-
ists, they are adapted to a particular niche. There is no scientific
support for the notion that we have been propelled towards a pre-
determined end by a Divine Watchmaker or even a Blind one.

This is a non-intuitive result. However, many of the characteristic human features (brain size, hairlessness, prolonged adolescence)
can be attributed to a neotenous change[66] in the human line, which
could be genetically simple – perhaps the result of a single mutation. Furthermore, the complexity of language is a key human
characteristic, without denying or denigrating the sophistication
of communication in many non-human groups. The differentiating feature between ape and human is not the ability simply to
make sounds, but to control those sounds precisely. 'The missing
ingredient [which prevented the chimps developing more complex
speech] may have been a tiny change in anatomy of the proto-
human vocal tract to give us finer control and permit formation of
a much greater variety of sounds.'[67]

Alfred Russel Wallace argued that natural selection had acted in
the earlier stages of human differentiation from the apes, but as our
intellectual and moral faculties became 'fairly developed', the body
ceased to be subject to selection, and subsequently adaptation was
solely 'through the action of the mind'. Wallace's starting point was
a belief that brain size was a reliable indicator of mental capacities.
The difficulty as he saw it was that both fossil humans and 'savages'
had skulls (and therefore brains) of similar size to those of civilized

---

66. The retention of juvenile features into adult life as a result of the rate of
    maturation slowing.
67. J. Diamond, *The Rise and Fall of the Third Chimpanzee* (London: Radius,
    1991), p. 47.

people, and consequently all must be presumed to have the same mental capacities. However it seemed to Wallace that such traits as mathematical ability and the ability to carry out complex trains of abstract reasoning would been useless (if not harmful) in the struggle for existence in primitive cultures. As it was both unneeded and unused, the brain could not have evolved by natural selection alone. Consequently, and certainly influenced by his belief in spiritualism, he proposed that a 'Higher Intelligence' had guided human evolution in 'definite direction and for special ends'.

Darwin disagreed with Wallace's conclusion that 'natural selection could not have done it all', but he was himself unsure how selection might have acted to produce morality. He wrote in the *Descent of Man*: 'He who was ready to sacrifice his life, as many a savage has been, rather than betray his colleagues, would often leave no offspring to inherit his noble nature.'[68] An answer to this problem could be if a group rather than an individual is the target of selection, and there have been repeated proposals for group selection.[69] However, this seems highly improbable from all that we know about biological fitness and gene transmission.

It was left to J. B. S. Haldane (1932) to show a way forward, pointing out that if individual unselfishness (even to the extent of self-sacrifice) had an inherited basis and helped near relatives, then 'altruistic genes' could be selected and therefore spread within families.[70] In this way, there could be situations where cooperation

---

68. London: John Murray, 1871, p. 200.
69. For example: D. S. Wilson, *Darwin's Cathedral: Evolution, Religion and the Nature of Society* (Chicago: Chicago University Press, 2002); L. A. Dugatkin, *The Altruism Equation* (Princeton: Princeton University Press, 2006).
70. He first put forward this idea in his 1932 book (*Causes of Evolution*, n. 54), but presented it in a more popular form in an article in 1955. 'Let us suppose that you carry a rare gene which affects your behaviour so that you jump into a flooded river and save a child, but you have one chance in ten of being killed, while I do not possess the gene and stand on the bank and watch the child drown. If the child is your own child or your brother or sister, there is an even chance that the child will also have this

(or unselfishness) is an advantage to a group of individuals, even if particular individuals are disadvantaged. Haldane's argument was formalized in 1964 by W. D. Hamilton as 'inclusive fitness', often called nowadays 'kin selection', and popularized by E. O. Wilson (1975) as 'sociobiology'.[71] Sociobiological ideas have been extremely important in biology, and have stimulated an immense amount of research. They have also provoked much dissent, particularly as they apply to mammals (especially humankind) because of the implications that behavioural choices are programmed (or determined) by genes.

Our ancestry has certainly been shaped by selection. However, this does not mean that we will fully understand human nature even if we successfully bring together embryology, anatomy, genetics, ecology and behavioural studies. Certainly such a synthesis is a necessary preliminary step, but it would be foolish to expect this to give us all the answers we would like, even if we could develop a rational synthesis. Nor do we have to go along with Wallace and postulate a guiding 'Higher Intelligence'. But before we can proceed, we have to respond to the arch-reductionists who insist that we are no more than survival machines controlled by selfish genes and those who focus on personal and sexual relationships and group dynamics. E. O. Wilson, prophet of a middle road, argues that there are two sorts of people, empiricists and transcendentalists, and that the

---

Footnote 70 (*cont.*)

gene, so five genes will be saved in children for one lost in an adult. If you save a grandchild or nephew, the advantage is only two and a half to one. If you only save a first cousin, the effect is very slight. If you try to save your first cousin once removed the population is more likely to lose this valuable gene than to gain it . . . It is clear that genes making for conduct of this kind would only have a chance of spreading in rather small populations where most of the children were fairly near relatives of the man who risked his life' ('Population Genetics', *New Biology* 18 [1955], pp. 34–51, p. 44).

71. W. D. Hamilton, 'The Genetical Evolution of Social Behaviour', *Journal of Theoretical Biology* 7 (1964), pp. 1–52; E. O. Wilson, *Sociobiology* (Cambridge, MA: Harvard University Press, 1975).

robustness of this bi-polarity is testable 'by the continuance of biological studies of complex human behaviour'.[72]

Wilson has been pilloried as a modern high priest of naturalism,
giving insight to disciples such as Dawkins and Dennett. Wilson
wrote: 'What was the origin of mind, the essence of mankind?
We suggest that a very special form of evolution, the melding of
genetic change with cultural history, both created the mind and
drove the growth of the brain and the human intellect forward
. . . [we want to] link the research on gene-culture coevolution to
other, primarily anatomical studies of human evolution.'[73] On the
face of it, there is nothing particularly radical in this. Any evolution is the result of interactions between the environment – which
includes social forces – and the genetic system. The problems arise
when biology shades into theology.

Theologians from the most conservative to the most liberal
have struggled to explain – or even merely to describe – the
special nature of humankind in the face of evolutionary science.[74]
Humans are obviously different to the apes in many ways – but
are the differences merely ones of degree or is there a real qualitative difference? This is probably unanswerable from the scientific
point of view, but theologically there is a simple solution: to regard
the biological species *Homo sapiens,* descended from a primitive
simian stock and related to living apes, as having been transformed
by God at some time in history into *Homo divinus,* biologically
unchanged but spiritually distinct.[75] There is no reason to insist that
this event took place at the same time as the emergence of the biological form we call *H. sapiens*; it was not a genetic change. Genesis
I describes the appearance of *H. divinus* as a *bārā'* event, a specific

72. E. O. Wilson, *Consilience* (New York: Knopf, 1998), p. 264.

73. C. J. Lumsden and E. O. Wilson, *Promethean Fire. Reflections on the Origin of
      Mind* (Cambridge, MA: Harvard University Press, 1983), p. v.

74. J. R. Middleton, *The Liberating Image. The* imago Dei *in Genesis I* (Grand
      Rapids: Brazos Press, 2005).

75. J. R. W. Stott, *Understanding the Bible* (London: Scripture Union, 1972);
      R. J. Berry, 'This Cursed Earth. Is "the Fall" Credible?' *Science and Christian
      Belief* 11 (1999), pp. 29–49, 165–167.

act of God, while Genesis 2:7 describes it as a divine in-breathing into an already existing entity. Scriptural exegesis and modern neurobiology join in rejecting the notion that this is the addition of a soul to a body.[76] For Claus Westermann: 'The relationship to God is not something which is added to human existence; humans are created in such a way that their very existence is intended to be their relationship to God';[77] in the Genesis account, only 'the man' is addressed directly by God (Gen. 1:28). H. D. MacDonald comes down firmly on the conclusion that 'image should be taken as indicating sonship', seeing this as holding together both the ontological and relational aspects of the image.[78]

Can we distinguish between humanness (i.e. the acquisition of the *imago Dei*) emerging gradually and its instantaneous 'instatiation' by God? (I use the word 'instatiation' to avoid the mechanical implication of words such as 'insertion' or 'implanting'). Does the distinction matter? Genesis 1 uses two different Hebrew words to describe God's creative work: *'āśâ* (which has the sense of modelling from previous material, as a potter moulds clay) and *bārā'* which is used to refer to the creation of matter (v. 1), the great sea monsters (v. 21) and mankind (v. 26), and which is always used in the Bible to refer to God's creative activity. It would be dangerous to build too much on this use of words. Both refer to a divine work and there is no clear demarcation in the Bible between God's works in nature and his works in history; he is sovereign in both.[79] But as Westermann comments,

---

76. W. S. Brown, N. Murphy and H. N. Malony (eds.), *Whatever Happened To the Soul?* (Minneapolis: Fortress Press, 1998); M. A. Jeeves, 'Towards a Composite Portrait of Human Nature', in M. A. Jeeves (ed.), *From Cells to Souls – and Beyond* (Grand Rapids: Eerdmans, 1998), pp. 233–249.

77. Claus Westermann, *Genesis 1–11*, transl. J. J. Scullion (London: SPCK, 1984), p. 158.

78. H. D. MacDonald, *The Christian View of Man* (London: Marshall, Morgan and Scott, 1981), pp. 39–41.

79. O. R. Barclay, 'Design In Nature', *Science and Christian Belief* 18 (2006), pp. 49–61.

the meaning is indisputable. Man in his entirety . . . is to be designated as a creature in God's image . . . [It] serves to underline the uniqueness of man's creation. The creation of man is something far different from the creation of the rest of the world. One can almost say that this ruptures the framework of the course of creation in which all the other works of creation are included.[80]

Was Adam an individual?

Did God make a single person (or pair) in his image, or did his image appear in a group of individuals? [81] Certainly the word translated 'Adam' may be taken to mean collective humanity. James Dunn probably speaks for most interpreters when he writes of Paul's use in Romans 5:12 of the 'one man' by whom sin came into

80. Westermann, *The Genesis Accounts of Creation*, transl. N. E. Wagner (Philadelphia: Fortress, 1964), p. 21.

81. The human species has gone through various bottlenecks in number through its history, as shown by the low genetic variability of some populations. A particularly significant bottleneck was the migration out of Africa, with modern African populations showing much greater inherited variation (notably in mitochondrial types, which are transmitted wholly through the female line), than extra-Africans, who have very little mitochondrial variation (R. L. Cann, M. Stoneking and A. C. Wilson, 'Mitochondrial DNA and Human Evolution', *Nature* 325 [1987], pp. 31–36). The common female ancestor of all these mitochondrial lines has been called 'mitochondrial Eve', but she should not be equated with the biblical Eve. All that is implied is that mitochondrial Eve has had an unbroken line of female descendants (B. Sykes, *Seven Daughters of Eve* [London: Bantam Press, 2001]). Based on the rate of differentiation of existing population groups, mitochondrial Eve lived around 200,000 years ago (L. Loewe and S. Scherer, 'Mitochondrial Eve: The Plot Thickens', *Trends in Ecology and Evolution* 12 [1997], pp. 422–423), which accords well with the palaeontological findings of migration from Africa. If the 'biblical Adam and Eve' truly lived in the Neolithic era as the Genesis text implies (Gen. 2:15; 4:2, 17, 22), they would have been around ten to twenty thousand years ago.

the world: 'in introducing the drama in these terms, Paul indicated he wants this figure to be seen not so much as an individual in his own right, but as more than an individual figure, what we might call an "epochal figure" – that is, as one who initiated the first major phase of human history and thereby determined the character of that phase for those belonging to it.'[82]

Notwithstanding, the suggestion that there was no 'historic Adam' is wholly unacceptable to many.[83] Indeed, contemporary 'creationism' stems from the cry 'No Adam, no Fall; no Fall, no Atonement; no Atonement, no Savior', explicit in the teaching of the Adventist Ellen White and the writings of her followers, notably George McCready Price.[84] It is entirely separate from the scientific debates about Darwinism – a fact which goes a long way to explaining the bewilderment and expressions of irrelevance of most scientists when challenged about evolution. But the exegetical need for an historic Adam is demanded by many commentators. Perhaps surprisingly, James Barr argues for it on linguistic grounds. He points out that Paul makes much of the distinction in Galatians 3:16 between 'seed' or 'offspring' (singular) and 'seeds' (plural), and hence he would be unlikely to mean men (plural) in Romans 5 where he repeatedly speaks of 'one man'.[85] More conventionally, John Stott argues for the historicity of Adam:

> Scripture clearly intends us to accept their [Adam and Eve's] historicity as the original human pair: the biblical genealogies trace the human race back to Adam, Jesus himself taught that 'at the beginning the Creator made them male and female' and then instituted marriage, Paul told the

---

82. James Dunn, *Romans 1–8* (Word Biblical Commentary 38A; Dallas: Word, 1988), p. 289.

83. See Henri Blocher in this volume, ch. 7.

84. M. J. Cole, 'Scopes and Beyond: Antievolutionism and American Culture', in L. R. Godfrey (ed.), *Scientists Confront Creationism* (New York: Norton, 1983), p. 19; R. L. Numbers, *The Creationists* (New York: Alfred Knopf, 1992), p. xi.; Giberson, *Saving Darwin*, n. 21, pp. 58–59.

85. James Barr, *Biblical Faith and Natural Theology* (Oxford: Clarendon Press, 1993), p. 166.

Athenian philosophers that God had made every nation from 'one man', and in particular, Paul's carefully constructed analogy between Adam and Christ depends for its validity on the equal historicity of both.[86]

Leon Morris agrees with this interpretation. He asserts 'the one man [Adam] is very important and underlies the whole discussion [in Romans 5]. Twelve times in verses 12–19 we have the word *one*; repeatedly Paul refers to the one man Adam (and to one sin of that one man) and opposes to him (and it) the one man Jesus Christ (and his one world of grace). The one man and his sin and the one Saviour and his salvation are critical to the discussion.' Notwithstanding, he warns that 'Paul's argument in Romans 5 is very condensed and in all translations and comments we must allow for the possibility that Paul's meaning may at some point be other than we think'.[87]

Dunn discusses and rejects the possibility that Adam can be regarded as merely a representative man: 'Paul does not use *anthrōpos* here to characterize humankind as a whole; the concept of corporate responsibility is more of a hindrance than a help'; he cites H. W. Robinson and F. F. Bruce in support.[88] However, *contra* John Stott, he argues that 'Paul's theological point [in Rom. 5] does not depend on Adam being a "historical" individual or on his disobedience being a historical event as such. Such an implication does not necessarily follow from the fact that a parallel is drawn from Christ's single act: an act in mythic history can be paralleled to an act in living history without the point of the comparison being lost.'[89]

Resolution of this point must be left to theological debate. However science can contribute on two points. The '*imago*' is as intrinsic part of humanness as eye colour or memory, but it would be wrong to assume that it is inherited or transmitted like a Mendelian trait. If it was initially conferred on an individual, there is no reason why it should not spread by divine *fiat* to all other members of *Homo*

---

86. J. R. W. Stott, *The Message of Romans* (BST; Leicester: IVP, 1994), p. 163.

87. Leon Morris, *The Epistle to the Romans* (Leicester: IVP, 1988), p. 228.

88. Dunn, *Romans 1–8*, p. 272.

89. Ibid., n. 88, p. 289.

sapiens alive at the time. Likewise, the effects of the disobedience of the first pair could also have spread 'laterally', a suggestion made by Derek Kidner in his Tyndale commentary on Genesis.[90] This understanding would emphasize the responsibility of individuals to respond to God in obedience, whereas interpreting 'Adam' as corporate humanity minimizes personal commitment and the consequences of disobedience.[91] Secondly, the 'death' that entered the world 'the day that Adam sinned' was, of course, primarily separation from God (e.g. Eph. 2:1–5), a rupture of relationship. Physical death was part of creation from the beginning, explicit in the Creator's provision of plants for animals to eat (Gen. 1:29, 30; 2:16).

Mankind-made-in-the-image-of-God (*Homo divinus*) is a creature

---

90. D. Kidner, *Genesis* (TOTC; Leicester: IVP, 1967), p. 29; see also Berry, 'This Cursed Earth', n. 75.

91. Neil Messer (*Selfish Genes and Christian Ethics* [London: SCM, 2007], p. 186) wonders why 'if each of Adam's contemporaries had God's image individually breathed into him or her, Adam's original sin had to go on to infect all members of the species. In other words, Berry's account can certainly do justice to the contingency of original sin (Adam and Eve's first sin was a freely willed choice), but it is far less clear that it can give a satisfactory account of its radicality, communicability or universality.' John Bimson ('Doctrines of the Fall and Sin after Darwin', in M. Northcott and R. J. Berry (eds.), *Theology After Darwin* [Carlisle: Paternoster, 2009]) also queries the federal headship notion, on the grounds that 'the name Adam gives to his wife ("Eve, because she was the mother of all living") and the genealogies in Gen 4 & 5 do seem to portray Adam as ancestor, not simple "federal head"'. None of these objections are necessarily fatal to the federal headship idea. Henri Blocher discusses the issue at length and concludes 'the decisive consideration when we search for the rightness of the "fact" [of being born sinners] remains the headship or capitate structure – the organic solidarity of the race, the spiritual dimension of humanity's oneness' (*Original Sin* [Leicester: Apollos, 1997], p. 129). He accepts that his view differs from the 'current headship solution' but he clearly does not reject the concept. I am not competent to argue this point, but I want to insist that the model I have proposed remains viable, although it may require nuancing.

in relationship with God. Although the creative acts of God are described throughout Genesis 1 as divinely driven processes ('Let there be. . .'), in Genesis 1:26 (only), the text is explicitly personal: 'Let *us* make human beings. . .'; in verse 29 God addresses the newly created humans as 'you'. The 'image of God' means that we are sufficiently like God that we can have an intimate relationship with him: we are told that God walks in the garden with Adam and Eve, and he speaks to them personally, in a different way to the rest of creation. The woman was created as an equal partner to Adam because 'it was not good for the man to be alone'. The 'Fall' story describes a multiple break in relationships: Adam and Eve were scared and hid from God; tense with each other; and alienated from the non-human creation.

A common theological understanding of the evolving ape which became humankind, is that the 'temptation story' in Genesis 3 is merely a way of describing the advent of self-awareness; the eating of the fruit which led to 'the opening of the eyes' of our first parents refers to the development of conscience and the possibility of moral choice. In these terms, the 'Fall' becomes an upward leap into true humanness rather than a descent into moral turpitude. Julian Huxley used to speak of us of having moved from the biological phase of evolution into what he called the 'psychosocial phase'; C. H. Waddington described it as the 'sociogenetic phase'. Teilhard de Chardin's idea of progress towards 'omega point' expressed a similar notion.

It is almost trite to point out that there is no evidence whatsoever that we are improving morally in any respect. But the problem of positing an 'upward Fall' is the damage that it does to the biblical meta-narrative. The most often repeated description of Christ's accomplishment in redemption is that he 'delivered us from death': 'You once were dead because of your sins and wickedness . . . but God brought us to life with Christ when we were dead because of our sins' (Eph. 2:1, 5)[92]; 'Although you were dead because of your sins . . . he has brought you to life with Christ' (Col. 2:13); 'We know we have crossed over from death to life' (1 John 3:14); it is implicit in our Lord's conversation with Nicodemus about being 'born

---

92. All Bible quotations in this chapter are REB.

again' (recorded in John 3:1–14). In the context, 'death' cannot be physical death, nor can it be simply a figure of speech (as in the parable of the Prodigal Son: 'My son was dead', Luke 15:32); it must mean spiritual death in the sense of being separated from God – the fate Adam and Eve suffered when they were banished from Eden.

The language and imagery of 'death' might imply that physical and spiritual death are the same, but we should resist this. The death from which Christ saved us is not simply spiritual insensitivity or blindness, nor is it merely a liability to physical mortality; it is a severance of relationship with God, the source of life. Interestingly William Buckland suggested as early as 1837 in his Bridgewater Treatise that human death ought to be distinguished from animal (i.e. biological) death.[93] The deciding factor for him was the vast numbers of previously living organisms represented only by fossils. Challenged about this, he preached a sermon before the University of Oxford on Romans 5:12: 'It was through one man that sin entered the world and through sin death, and thus death pervaded the whole human race, inasmuch as all have sinned.'

Distinguishing between biological and spiritual death could be regarded as importing a dualism into humanness, but it is a very weak version of dualism; in no way does it represent 'body' and 'soul' as separate entities as in the classical dualism of Plato or Descartes. Charles Moule has argued that there is indeed a dualism in Paul's thought, but it is one between filial obedience and disobedience.[94] This gives independent support to the understanding about death as a lack of relationship because it buttresses the interpretation of our divinely given humanness as being essentially about relationships.

The 'sin that led to death' (Rom. 5:12) was, of course, Adam's disobedience in Eden. It is does not seem too far-fetched to note that Adam's failure was at root a failure of stewardship, disregarding the very first command to the human race and hence ignoring the purpose for which we were placed on earth; at one level, eating

---

93. W. Buckland, *Geology and Mineralogy Considered with Relation to Natural Theology* (London: William Pickering, 1837).

94. Charles Moule, 'St Paul and Dualism: the Pauline Conception of Resurrection', *New Testament Studies* 13 (1965–6), pp. 106–123.

the forbidden fruit was simple disobedience, but its significance was treating God as unnecessary and irrelevant.

The effects of the Fall

What were the effects of Adam's disobedience? The most relevant commentary on the consequences of the 'Fall' described in Genesis 3 is in Romans 8:19–22, where the created universe is said to have been 'made subject to frustration' and to be 'groaning as if in the pangs of childbirth'. It is a difficult passage. As Dunn points out, at one level it 'recalls the extent to which believers continue to be thoroughly bound up with creation, and that precisely as part of and not despite the process of salvation'. [95] But this is only part of it. Commenting on the Genesis story, Derek Kidner contrasts the pre-Fall situation with our present existence: 'Leaderless, the choir of creation can only grind on in discord. It seems from Romans 8:19–23 and from what is known of the pre-human world that there was a state of travail from the first which man was empowered to "subdue" until he relapsed into disorder himself.' [96]

Charles Cranfield has used the same analogy with a powerful *reductio ad absurdum* argument:

> What sense can there be in saying that the 'sub-human creation – the Jungfrau, for example, or the Matterhorn, or the planet Venus – suffers frustration by being prevented from properly fulfilling the purpose of its existence?' The answer must surely be that the whole magnificent theatre of the universe, together with all its splendid properties and all the varied chorus of sub-human life, created for God's glory, is cheated of its true fulfilment so long as man, the chief actor in the great drama of God's praise, fails to contribute his rational part. The Jungfrau and the Matterhorn and the planet Venus and all living things too, man alone excepted, do indeed

---

95. James Dunn, 'Spirit Speech: Reflections on Romans 8:12–27', in S. K. Soderlund and N. T. Wright (eds.), *Romans and the People of God* (Grand Rapids: Eerdmans, 1999), p. 88.
96. Kidner, *Genesis,* n. 90, p.73.

glorify God in their own ways; but since their praise is destined to be not a collection of individual offerings but part of a magnificent whole, the united praise of the whole creation, they are prevented from being fully that which they were created to be, so long as man's part is missing, just as all the other players in a concerto would be frustrated of their purpose if the soloist were to fail to play his part.[97]

Henri Blocher makes essentially the same point, 'If man obeys God, he would be the means of blessing the earth, but in his insatiable greed . . . and in his short-sighted selfishness, he pollutes the earth and destroys it. He turns a garden into a desert (cf. Rev 11:18). That is the main thrust of the curse of Genesis 3.'[98]

The Fall is not primarily about disease and disaster, nor about the dawn of self-awareness. Rather it is a way of describing the fracture in relationship between God and the human creature made in his image.[99] The rupture means that we rattle around in our space, as it were, producing disorder within ourselves, with our neighbours, and with our environment (human and non-human). This will continue until our relationship with God is restored and we become 'at peace with God through our Lord Jesus who has given us access to the grace in which we now live; and we exult in the divine glory which is to be ours' (Rom. 5:1–2) – words which condition and explain the state of nature which Paul uses later in the same passage (Rom. 8:19–21). This is the point where we converge on Southgate's defence of divine teleology in creation through humans having a crucial role as 'created co-creators' with God, rather than through the classical and persistent tradition of ingenuous anthropocentrism.[100]

---

97. Charles Cranfield, 'Some Observations on Romans 8:19–21', in R. Banks (ed.), *Reconciliation and Hope: New Testament Essays on Atonement and Eschatology Presented to L. L. Morris on his 60th Birthday* (Grand Rapids: Eerdmans, 1974), p. 227.

98. H. Blocher, *In the Beginning* (Leicester: IVP, 1984), p. 184.

99. J. J. Bimson, 'Reconsidering a "'cosmic fall'"', *Science and Christian Belief* 18 (2006), pp. 63–81.

100. C. C. B. Southgate, 'God and Evolutionary Evil: Theodicy in the Light of Darwinism', *Zygon* 37 (2002), pp. 803–821.

An obvious implication of the Fall is that it highlights the need for restoring the break in our relationship with God. The possibility of this is, of course, the gospel: we are assured that God, through Christ, has 'reconciled *all things* to himself, making peace through the shedding of his blood on the cross' (Col. 1:20). C. F. D. Moule has commented that Romans 8:19–21 means that 'man is responsible before God for nature. As long as man refuses to play the part assigned him by God, so long the entire world of nature is frustrated and dislocated. It is only when man is truly fitting into his proper position as a son in relation to God his Father that the dislocation of nature will be reduced.'[101]

From beginning to end, the Bible speaks of our interdependence with the rest of creation. There is no hint of distinct 'magisteria' as suggested by Stephen Gould.[102] Sometimes we are given direct commands, as when we are told to 'have dominion'; in other places, the instructions are implicit (the perils of a journey, the care needed for a farm or a flock of animals, the mastery we may expect over wild animals or fierce weather). We are told that sin led to Noah's flood and also to drought (Lev. 26:14–26; Deut. 28:15–24); the food laws regulated hunting; a very positive attitude to creation is expressed in the Wisdom Literature. Increasingly we are learning how much we depend upon 'creation's [nature's] services'.[103] In all cases we interact with creation; we are a part of it as well as apart from it. But throughout is a parallel theme: that this is God's world, that he has made a covenant with us which he has promised to uphold, and that both creation and ourselves were reconciled to God by Christ's death on the cross.

101. C. F. D. Moule, *Man and Nature in the New Testament* (London: Athlone Press, 1964), p. 12.

102. Stephen Gould, *Rocks of Ages* (New York: Ballantine, 1999).

103. R. Constanza, R. d'Arge, R. deGroot, *et al.*, 'The Value of the World's Ecosystem Services and Natural Capital', *Nature* 387 (1997), pp. 254–260. Millennium Ecosystem Assessment, *Ecosystems and Human Well-being: General Synthesis* (New York: World Resources Institute, 2005).

Conclusion

The Fall is the place above all where biology and theology conflict. The commonest evasion of this is to rewrite theology.[104] For example, Patricia Williams in a book-length treatment concludes

> both the literal and liberal interpretations of the narrative of Adam and
> Eve have collapsed: The reputed historicity [of Adam and Eve] conflicts
> with well-established scientific theories . . . Science says the claim liberal
> theology inherited from literalism, that we are alienated and exiled is
> false . . . the concept of alienation is recent. It arrived with agricultural
> surpluses and class distinctions about ten thousand years ago . . . Jesus
> shows that we are not alienated from God, but live in God's presence.[105]

This heterodox interpretation of the human condition is unlikely to be shared by many Christians – certainly not those who accept the authority of Scripture.

A more widespread problem is the widespread occurrence of conflict and death in the natural world. Could a good God have created this?[106] There has been much discussion of this point.[107] It

---

104. See Bowler, *Monkey Trials*, n. 1.

105. Patricia Williams, *Doing without Adam and Eve. Sociobiology and Original Sin* (Minneapolis: Fortress Press, 2002), pp. 199–200.

106. In a review of Phillip Johnson's purported defence of orthodox Christianity by attacking evolutionary 'naturalism' (*Darwin on Trial* [Washington DC: Regnery Gateway, 1991]), David Hull wrote: 'What kind of God can one infer from the sort of phenomena epitomised by the species on Darwin's Galapagos Islands? The evolutionary process is rife with happenstance, contingency, incredible waste, death, pain and horror . . . Whatever the God implied by evolutionary theory and the data of natural selection may be like, he is not the Protestant God of waste not, want not. He is also not even the awful God portrayed in the Book of Job. The God of the Galapagos is careless, wasteful, indifferent, almost diabolical. He is certainly not the sort of God to whom anyone would be inclined to pray' ('God of the Galapagos', *Nature* 352 [1991], p. 485).

107. See, for example M. Ruse, *Can a Darwinian be a Christian?* (Cambridge:

is an extremely important issue, but is somewhat peripheral to this essay. Indeed, for most religious people (not only Christians), the sticking point about human evolution is probably not the existence of 'nature red in tooth and claw', but the idea that humans are nothing more than upgraded monkeys and not individuals specially created in God's image. The contemporary fashion in many evangelical circles for 'intelligent design' can be regarded in part as an attempt to escape this dilemma, but it does not really help; indeed the concept of 'Intelligent Design' as currently formulated does not withstand critical scrutiny well[108] – at best it can be regarded as little more than Deism reborn. The issue is not design as such. Whether or not they are evolutionists, Christians and Muslims fully accept that the world is the result of design by an omnipotent Creator.

The seduction of intelligent design is that it seems to avoid the assumed godless materialism of Darwinism and therefore apparently provides a way forward for Christians unhappy about the apparent naivety of traditional six-day creationism. Nonetheless it fails satisfactorily to bring together Scripture with scientific understanding of the real world.[109] While the God revealed in Scripture is not limited by the mechanisms that he has made, he normally

---

Cambridge University Press, 2001); Southgate, 'God and Evolutionary Evil', n. 99, and idem, *The Groaning of Creation* (Edinburgh: Alban Books, 2008).

108. F. J. Ayala, *Darwin and Intelligent Design* (Minneapolis: Fortress, 2006), P. Kitcher, *Living with Darwin* (New York: Oxford University Press, 2007). The claim by Michael Behe (*Darwin's Black Box* [New York: Free Press, 1996]; *The Edge of Evolution* [New York: Free Press, 2007]) that some organs are too 'irreducibily complex' to have evolved by Darwinian mechanisms has been widely rejected. See J. A. Coyne, 'God in the Details', *Nature* 383 (1997), pp. 227–228; T. Cavalier-Smith, 'The Blind Biochemist', *Trends in Ecology and Evolution* 12 (1997), pp. 162–163; H. A. Orr, 'Darwin v. Intelligent Design (Again)', *Boston Review* 21 (2007); K. R. Miller, *Finding Darwin's God* (New York: HarperCollins, 1999); idem, 'Falling Over the Edge', *Nature* 447 (2007), pp. 1055–1056.

109. D. Alexander, *Creation or Evolution. Do We Have To Choose?* (Oxford: Monarch, 2008), ch. 15.

works through them: he 'feeds the birds' and 'clothes the grass in the fields' (Matt. 6:26, 30) through processes we can investigate. All things hold together in him: he is immanent as well as transcendent. There are challenges in the evolutionary process, but no intrinsic reason why the God who made matter out of nothing and progressively transformed it from chaos to order should not mainly work through processes that we can study by the usual methods of observation and experiment. There is wonder in being able, in Kepler's words, 'to think God's thoughts after him'.

Darwin died on 19 April 1882 and was buried in Westminster Abbey. Frederick Bridge, the Abbey organist, composed an anthem for the occasion based on Proverbs 3:13–17: 'Happy is the man that findeth wisdom and getteth understanding. She is more precious than rubies and all the things that thou canst desire are not to be compared unto her. Length of days is in her right hand and in her left hand riches and honour. Her ways are ways of pleasantness and all her paths are peace.'

Darwin certainly gave wisdom and coherence to fragmented understandings of the natural world. The sadness is that so many have found discord and disharmony in his legacy.

© R. J. Berry, 2009

3. THEOLOGICAL CHALLENGES FACED BY DARWIN

Darrel R. Falk

Evolution, God and suffering

Following the discovery of his theory, Darwin was deeply concerned about the incongruence of a benevolent, omnipotent, omniscient God bringing new life through a process that included pain, suffering and competition-for-survival. He came to believe that his theory was inconsistent with belief in a God of that sort, as evidenced, for example, by these statements in letters. The first was written in 1856 to J. D. Hooker and the second to Asa Gray in 1860:

> What a book a Devil's chaplain might write on the clumsy, wasteful, blundering low and horridly cruel works of nature.[1]

> There seems to me to be too much misery in the world. I cannot persuade myself that a beneficent & omnipotent God would have

---

1. In F. Burkhardt and S. Smith (eds.), *The Correspondence of Charles Darwin 1844–1846*, vol. 6 (Cambidge: Cambridge Univesity Press, 1987), p. 178.

designedly created the Ichneumonidae with the express intention of their feeding within the living bodies of caterpillars, or that a cat should play with mice.[2]

There is nothing particularly new about this challenge that confronted Darwin. We live in a world of pain and suffering. It should not surprise us and probably should not have 'bewildered' Darwin that the story of creation is interwoven with a story of suffering.[3] From the human perspective all of us would like to remove suffering from that story. We would like to remove suffering from *our* story. So, 150 years later, there is a sense in which we can identify with Darwin's dilemma. But it is not a new problem that began with Darwinian insights. We have a whole book of the Bible that focuses exclusively on the problem of pain and suffering, devoting forty-two chapters to it – the book of Job. For thirty-seven chapters, Job cries out to God in distress and anger about the apparent injustice of suffering. In the thirty-eighth chapter, Job begins to listen.

The climax of the book comes when Job is finally confronted with human naïveté in light of the mystery of God's ways in the universe. Job speaks for all believers through the ages when he concludes 'Surely I spoke of things I did not understand, things too wonderful for me to know . . . my ears had heard of you but now my eyes have seen you' (Job 42:3, 5).[4]

What had those eyes come to see? Did they not simply come to see the reality of God's presence? Did his mind not simply come to trust in that presence despite his inability to comprehend the problem of suffering?

Perhaps, from the theological perspective, Darwin was simply asking the question of the ages. From that viewpoint, Darwin

---

2. Letter 2814, 22 May 1860 <http://www.darwinproject.ac.uk/ darwinletters/calendar/entry-2814.html>.

3. In the above letter to Gray, Darwin expresses bewilderment and indicates that in light of his observations he cannot see 'evidence of design and beneficence on all sides of us'.

4. All Bible quotations unless otherwise indicated are NIV.

had not unlocked a new question at all. As Darwin completed his theory of evolution, perhaps the issue was that he, unlike Job, never made it to the thirty-eighth chapter, where Job *listened* while God spoke to him.[5]

Suffering exists not just in the history of the evolution of new life forms, it has always existed in everyday life as well. We must not downplay suffering, whether in the emergence of new life forms in evolution, or in the suffering that exists through seemingly stochastic events associated with disease or accidents. Suffering is a side effect of the freedom that God wills for creation. When we romanticize creation as being the work of an engineer who pre-ordains every detail rather than the work of a God who builds freedom into creation, we point to a reality that doesn't exist.

If there is any one message to be derived from the entire ongoing saga of the interaction between God and the Hebrew people as they wandered for forty years through the desert, it is that God chooses to work through an interplay between *freedom* and *necessity*. God certainly did not dictate the wanderers' every move. He gave them a high level of freedom as they wandered around, making their own choices and suffering on occasion as a consequence of that freedom. But in the midst of this freedom was the overarching premise that God had chosen a people and God was leading them on their journey to the Promised Land. Darwin's discovery of the freedom granted to creation as a whole mirrors the freedom that God grants to human beings in their sojourn on earth. However, just as God's subtle presence guides the life of a follower of God in the journey to the Promised Land, so God's subtle presence in creation is the Logos who is before all things

---

5. It is important to point out though, that Darwin did end his letter to Gray with a statement that resembles Job's final willingness to acquiesce in the mystery of divine action: 'I feel most deeply that the whole subject is too profound for the human intellect. A dog might as well speculate on the mind of Newton. – Let each man hope & believe what he can.' In light of his theory, Darwin seemed unable to hope for, unable to believe in, and unable to accept the notion of a benevolent God who is at work in creation.

and through whom everything in the universe is held together.[6] There is a grandeur in this view of creation that parallels that which we experience in our own lives. We experience freedom; creation as a whole clearly experiences freedom as well. But as believers, we live out that freedom in the necessity of God's guiding presence; the same is true for creation as a whole.

Where Christians fail to recognize this interplay between freedom and necessity in their own lives, and where they fail to recognize this same interplay in the story of an evolving creation, they become responsible for perpetuating Darwin's dilemma in our own twenty-first-century world. God wills freedom for our lives and God wills freedom for creation; suffering is a by-product of freedom, but suffering does not remove us from the Logos who is in all, through all, and above all.

Has our understanding of pain and suffering progressed much beyond where it was left in the forty-second chapter of Job, two and half thousand years ago? Not really. The details of the answer are hidden somewhere in the mystery of the dialectic between a loving God who wills freedom for creation and the same loving God who is sovereign; a God who Job finally came to worship despite his ignorance. The fact is that in the midst of pain and suffering in our world, beauty keeps peeking through. This world is incredibly beautiful, but that beauty has come about through pain and turmoil. The story of creation, as Darwin discovered it, is no different than the world we see, as bad things happen to those we love. We never get an answer to the question of why it works this way except for the hints that it is embedded in God's will for freedom in this universe. Nonetheless, through hope, we get these glimpses of beauty and in those glimpses every now and then we're surprised by joy.

God's Spirit is at work within us as we struggle against the chaos. We can focus on the Spirit and what *emerges* from the chaos or we can focus on the chaos and lose sight of the Spirit who is at work. The choice is ours. Darwin chose to focus on the chaotic forces and assumed there was no Spirit at work. As believers, we focus on God's Spirit and what God's Spirit brings out of the

---

6. Col. 1:17.

chaos. Like Job, we don't understand why, but in faith we assume there is no other way.

So that's the first challenge that Darwin faced in light of evolution: the reality of the fact that new species emerged from suffering. Indeed, it depended on that suffering. In fact, it was the life-*giving* principle from which new life would emerge.

God's providence and randomness

The second theological challenge which deeply impacted Darwin related to the fact that he was deeply steeped in the thinking of William Paley's Design-Engineer – the God who worked out every detail of creation in advance. Paley was one of the most influential theologians of the Church of England at the time and Darwin, as a student at Cambridge University, had to pass an exam on Paley's *Evidences of Christianity* and *Moral and Political Philosophy*. He also went on to read *Natural Theology*, a book which made a deep impression on him. In his autobiography, Darwin wrote:

> The old argument of design in nature, as given by Paley, which formerly seemed to me so conclusive, fails, now that the law of natural selection has been discovered. We can no longer argue that, for instance, the beautiful hinge of a bivalve shell must have been made by an intelligent being like the hinge of a door by man. There seems to be no more design in the variability of organic beings and in the action of natural selection, than in the course which the wind blows.[7]

Thus, as the years went by, he came to see that apparent random forces were at work in the natural world, and it caused his view of a 'Watchmaker-God' to come crashing down, broken into random pieces.

This question of whether God is present in events of life that may appear random is another issue that is not new to Charles

---

7. *The Autobiography of Charles Darwin*, ed. Nora Barlow (London: Collins, 1958), p. 87.

Darwin's discovery. The ancient Hebrews wrestled with this question just as they wrestled with the question of God's presence in the midst of suffering. 'Are events always as random as they appear?' they in essence asked. And with that, for example, they proceeded to tell us the story of Joseph who *just happens* to be thrown into a pit, a short time before some slave traders *just happen* to pass by on their way to Egypt. Some time later he *just happens* to be sent to jail where he *just happens* to meet up with someone who *just happens* to have connections to Pharaoh. Later this same person *just happens* to recall his association with Joseph when it *just happens* that Pharaoh is reflecting on a dream he has had. The story continues as it describes the famine and the arrival of the brothers, culminating in Joseph's magnificent words: 'You intended to harm me, but God intended it for good to accomplish what is now being done, the saving of many lives' (Gen. 50:20).

The issue of Providence in the midst of seemingly random events did not arise for the very first time when Darwin considered the history of life; it is at least as old as the history of the Hebrew nation. This is the biblical story of Israel's foundations. From their wandering through the desert, to David's life in the caves with Saul in hot pursuit, to the Babylonian exile, there was a guiding hand influencing the course of events. Providence was at work. Some of the greatest psalms (23, 105 and 107, for example) are reflections on that guiding Providence.

Today in the twenty-first century, when we as believers look back on the events of our own lives, many of us suspect that not all is as random as it first appears. We may recall the college we happened to attend, or the person we happened to meet seemingly by chance who became our spouse. Perhaps we recall the job we did or didn't get. The list goes on and on, and any of these events may have set our whole life upon a particular course that changed everything. To anyone looking on from the outside, the events which so influenced our lives may appear random, but given the presence of the Holy Spirit in our life as believers, many of us are not so sure. We look back on our lives and doubt that all is totally random and uninfluenced by Providence. The Twenty-Third Psalm is our story too. We see a guiding hand present in ways that are almost imperceptible were they not seen through the eyes of faith.

True, there is considerable difference of opinion amongst believers as to just how random events really are. Some go so far as to say nothing is random, it is all pre-ordained in some fashion. Others would indicate that God never interferes with the events in our lives. Whatever our perspective on this issue, as believers in Christ we conclude that God's Spirit is present with us in the events, no matter how random they appear or even no matter how random they really are.

If it had been possible to record a movie of life's history and we were to scan through it today, we would see a lot of 'just happened' events on life's journey towards humanness or any other trajectory life has taken. As believers we can accept that the history of life is an interplay between apparent randomness and the will of God. Some might even go so far as to say that God's will is simply to let randomness[8] play itself out, but always in God's presence and always in response to God's persuasive words, 'let there be life'. Others would say that God subtly (or perhaps not so subtly) influenced the processes of life's history in an ongoing interventional manner such that it was not random at all. Like the events of our lives, they would say it is difficult (perhaps impossible) to prove God's intervention even if we were really able to watch the movie and thereby dissect its progress. The latter (God's ongoing intervention) especially parallels the activity of the God of the Bible as God's people journey to the Promised Land and beyond, to Bethlehem, to Calvary, and eventually to the New Jerusalem.

The problem that Darwin brings up in the seemingly randomness-of-life's history is not a new problem and the fact that he *thought* it was is indicative of the inadequacies of the theology of his day – William Paley's natural theology. 'Apparent' randomness says nothing about whether a process is truly independent of an influence which supersedes that which we can measure using scientific tools. Because such tools are likely incapable of testing

---

8. Even this 'randomness' should not be thought truly random since it is contingent on God's ongoing presence and since the cascade of events in life's history were initiated not at random, but in response to God's command.

the statement which follows, Darwin had no basis, scientific or otherwise, for rejecting it; and there are very good logical reasons for accepting it:

> For by him [Christ] all things were created: things in heaven and on earth, visible and invisible, whether thrones or powers or rulers or authorities; all things were created by him and for him. He is before all things, and in him all things hold together (Col. 1:16–17).

Even seemingly random events always take place in a world governed by the immanence of God. Although we may not be able to prove this through scientific tools, we can do that one thing of which we are capable. Observing the beauty and majesty of the final product we can fall to our knees and worship the source of that beauty:

> Therefore I have uttered what I did not understand,
> things too wonderful for me, which I did not know . . .
> I had heard of you by the hearing of the ear,
> but now my eye sees you (Job 42:3, 5 NRSV).

The death of Darwin's daughter

The third issue for Darwin was the death, about seven years before the publication of the *Origin of Species*, of his ten-year-old beloved daughter Annie, most likely from tuberculosis. The events of this phase of his life have been clearly laid out in the book *Annie's Box*, by Charles' great-grandson, Randal Keynes. This issue, for Darwin, was not so much related to his biological discovery as to the sorts of events that all of us face. A terrible thing happened to someone whom he greatly loved, and he could never find anything more than a detached, non-benevolent God after Annie.

> After Annie's death, Charles set the Christian faith firmly behind him. He did not attend church services with the family; he walked with them to the church door, but left them to enter on their own . . . While others

had faith in God's infinite goodness, Charles found him a shadowy, inscrutable, ruthless figure.[9]

Of course the issue here is exactly the same as the tragedy of Job that we've already discussed. This time though, it was personal for Darwin. It is one thing to look out at the biological universe and say, I don't see how a loving Creator could create that way, it is quite another to feel the death-blow of one you love deeply. That event especially did not make theological sense to him.

In the ninth chapter of John's Gospel, Jesus and his disciples come across a man born blind. The disciples ask a deep theological question: in essence, why would this man have been born blind, who sinned to bring it about? What an important question they have posed, and in a sense the whole world waits with bated breath for Jesus to answer. So what does Jesus say? Actually, he simply healed the man. His answer was that bad things happen and we can work through those tragedies to make the world better. Just like the tragedy in the book of Job, God works alongside us to make our world better, but Jesus never tells us why it sometimes seems to blow up in our face. It is not always sin, we are told in both Job and John 9. In Job, his friends kept telling him to acknowledge his sin because that was clearly the cause of his suffering. In John, the disciples assumed that sin had brought about the man's blindness. So it was not sin in these two cases, and it is not always sin today. Rather, there is a strong hint in both passages that sometimes bad things are simply the natural outcome of a world embedded in freedom. The outcome, however, also takes place in a world deeply embedded in the love of God.

Conclusion

So, it is 150 years since *The Origin of Species*. We have an amazing amount of detail regarding the thoughts of the person who is likely

9. Randall Keynes, *Annie's Box* (London: Fourth Estate, 2001), p. 222.

the greatest biologist who ever lived. He was concerned that he saw no evidence for anything except randomness, when in fact he also saw no evidence *to rule out* a Creator who was present in the midst of what may not have been random at all. He was concerned that his theory dictated that the Creator worked through suffering to bring new life. And finally he was concerned that life itself as he experienced it was messy – full of ups and downs, with the downs causing him to believe that God was absent.

Sadly, what Darwin was rejecting was the natural theology of his youth, based around Paley's watchmaker hypothesis. Darwin ignores the massive amount of evidence which began accumulating long before his beautiful theory was ever composed: God is creating a universe deeply embedded in freedom. There is mystery in why the universe is being created in this way rather than the way we would do it if we were God. But we're not God, so instead all we can do is to follow the signposts that show through in the fog of our own inability to clearly understand. That's all we've ever had – just signposts in the mist. But Darwin, important as his theory may be, didn't knock down a single signpost. One hundred and fifty years later, the signposts are still standing. Sometimes it seems the lettering on the signposts flashes like neon. Other times, the fog created by our inability to understand blows in, enshrouding the signpost, and we have to strain to see the way. Darwin chose to focus on the fog that was made much more dense by his background in intelligent design theology.

So on the one hand Darwin was marvellously correct. Life has appeared on this earth in pretty much the way he pictured it. He was way ahead of his time with many of his ideas. Indeed he was way ahead of his time in his *epistemic* approach to biology. However, he was also terribly incorrect in other ways. He had uncovered no new theological barriers to faith. People had been wrestling with those questions for at least 2,500 years already. Some chose to believe *despite* the questions. Others chose to disbelieve *because* of the questions.

There was nothing particularly new, and the choice was Darwin's. The same choice is ours today – one hundred and fifty years after Darwin. We can focus on the fog as it drifts by, or we can focus on the signposts which point to a land where the tears are gone forever and where, in the light of the brightly shining Son, the fog of mystery will dissipate once and for all.[10]

© Darrel R. Falk, 2009

---

10. The metaphor used here is an extension of that used by C. S. Lewis in *Surprised By Joy* (New York: Harcourt Brace and World, Inc., 1955), p. 238.

4. GOD AND ORIGINS: INTERPRETING THE EARLY CHAPTERS OF GENESIS

Richard S. Hess

What does the Bible have to say about origins? We return to Genesis, and especially the first chapter of this fascinating book, to set the context for how early Israel would have understood the origins of the world.

For Christians and Jews who engage in the study of scientific evidence and theories for the origin of the world and life, the witness of the Scriptures is essential and raises questions of how it may or may not be related to the larger question. This is a matter of critical concern for those who believe these Scriptures to be inspired by the same God who created the universe. This study will briefly consider some of the major exegetical questions and purposes behind the creation account as described in Genesis 1:1 – 2:4. While other Old Testament texts are also important for the biblical study of creation (e.g., Job 38 – 39; many of the psalms; Isa. 40 – 45), Genesis 1 has received pride of place as the first text in the biblical record. Indeed, this passage is arguably the single most reflected upon written text ever written in human history. Thus its witness is worthy of consideration from the standpoint of the study of the humanities as well as from the perspective of questions of belief in universal and human origins.

This essay will consider five major aspects of this text.

- The overall message and context of Genesis 1:1 – 2:4 within the text of Genesis.
- A comparison of these verses with other creation stories to consider what is similar and what is distinctive about their message.[1]
- An examination of the summary of creation in Genesis 1:1 and the pre-creation description that comprises verse 2.
- A consideration of the creation of humanity described in verses 26–28.
- Some brief remarks on the overall structure, theology, and purpose of this account.

Throughout the study we will emphasize the literary and theological purposes of this text within the context of Hebrew literature and poetry. We will argue that neither traditional literalistic applications of this text to science nor dismissive 'symbolic' interpretations adequately appreciate the account and its intended message for either the first readers in ancient Israel or for modern readers today.

Context in Genesis

Genesis 1:1 – 2:4 should be understood as narrative form, as illustrated by the consistent use of the preterite (*waw* consecutive) tense that characterizes Hebrew narrative. The presence of repeated

---

1. For a summary of some useful studies on the literary and comparative analysis of the beginning chapters of Genesis, see Richard S. Hess and David Tsumura (eds.), *'I Studied Inscriptions From Before the Flood': Ancient Near Eastern, Linguistic and Literary Approaches to Genesis 1–11* (Sources for Biblical and Theological Study 4; Winona Lake: Eisenbrauns, 1994).

patterns in the days and various forms of divine command followed by a corresponding response suggest that this literature also partakes of Hebrew poetic styles. Such prose and poetry combinations are not unknown in Hebrew or Semitic literature, but they do require attention to the features of both kinds of literature.[2]

The overall story of Genesis 1:1 – 2:4 begins with a title or summary and is followed by a poetic description of the pre-creation state. There then appears a picture of the world created in six days in which the first three days set the background and context for the creation of life in days four through six. This abundant life fills the backgrounds of the first three days. Thus the first day describes the separation of light from darkness. This not only creates light but also allows for the sequence of time by distinguishing evening and morning, and night and day. The sun, moon, and stars are created to inhabit this space in day four. Their function is also described as marking off periods of time, such as months and years.

If day one corresponds to day four, day two relates to day five. On the second day the sky is separated from the waters above and below. The sky and the waters beneath it form homes for the birds and fish that are created on the fifth day. The third day sees the separation of dry land from the waters that are then formed into seas. Again, this corresponds to the creation of land animals and people on the sixth day. This structure demonstrates the close relationship between the first three days and the second three. The emphasis is on the creation of the contexts for life in the first

---

2. The bibliography is vast. See, for example, Robert Alter, *The Art of Biblical Narrative* (New York: Basic Books, 1981); J. P. Fokkelman, *Reading Biblical Poetry. An Introductory Guide* (Louisville: Westminster John Knox, 2001); Moshe Sternberg, *The Poetics of Biblical Narrative: Ideological Literature and the Drama of Reading* (Indianapolis: Indiana University Press, 1985). On the combination of poetry and prose in biblical and ancient Near Eastern literature, see Johannes C. de Moor and Wilfred G. E. Watson (eds.), *Verse in Ancient Near Eastern Prose* (Alter Orient und Altes Testament Band 42; Kevelaer: Butzon & Bercker and Neukirchen-Vluyn: Neukirchener, 1993).

half of the creation week. There follows the creation of life itself
in the second half. This life fills the creation. It is created in such
a manner as to honour the ongoing role of God in distinguishing and separating items: light from darkness, sky from water,
land from water, and now creatures from one another and after
their own kinds. The nature of the three areas and of the life that
inhabits them remains important in the priestly and ceremonial literature. One of the major distinctions between clean and unclean
animals, as defined in Leviticus 11, is that clean animals remain in
their sphere (sky, seas or land) and possess locomotion appropriate to that context.[3]

Genesis 2:4 identifies this account of the creation of the
heavens and the earth as *tôlĕdôt*. This term, derived from the
Hebrew root *yld* 'to bear, beget', introduces the genealogies of
Genesis in each of its remaining twelve occurrences. So we read
of the genealogy of Adam in 5:1 and of the genealogy of Shem in
11:10. Its occurrence in 2:4 positions the reference between the
two creation accounts of chapter one and chapter two. Although
it occurs elsewhere at the beginning of genealogies, its occurrence
here is not surprising because the reader would not understand
the use of *tôlĕdôt* at the beginning of chapter one. However, after
reading the whole account an Israelite reader would see what was
happening. There are no humans in Genesis 1 until the end of the
creation week. They cannot propagate the *tôlĕdôt* of the heaven
and the earth. On the other hand Genesis 1 would certainly avoid
references to something like the sun and moon giving birth to
the earth. This would invite polytheism, a danger to be avoided
at all costs. Instead, the author structures the creation account
by replacing the generations of the genealogies with the days of

---

3. Mary Douglas, *Purity and Danger* (London: Routledge & Keegan Paul,
   1966); idem, 'The Forbidden Animals in Leviticus', *Journal for the Study of
   the Old Testament* 59 (1993), pp. 3–23; idem, *Leviticus as Literature* (Oxford:
   Oxford University Press, 1999); Richard S. Hess, 'Leviticus', in T.
   Longman III and D. E .Garland (eds.), *The Expositor's Bible Commentary
   Revised Edition 1: Genesis–Leviticus* (Grand Rapids: Zondervan, 2008),
   pp. 568–569, 673–685.

creation. Rather than a chronological order, the result is a logical one in which each day prepares for the next and so anticipates or 'begets' it. Thus the days (Hebrew *yôm*) correspond to the generations of the other genealogies by forming a similar literary pattern, with their repeated references to evening and morning.[4]

In addition to beginning and corresponding to a literary pattern that structures the whole of Genesis, this *tôlĕdôt* form also provides an important theological insight. The *tôlĕdôt* traces the history of creation, humanity, and then the promised line through Abraham. It connects everything from the beginning of creation onward. Therefore it demonstrates that the God who created the world and everything in it is the same God who is in charge from the beginning until the present. Unlike other ancient Near Eastern accounts of theogony and other aspects of creation, these do not occur in a dreamlike time separated from the present in tone and expression. Rather, the creator God is the same God who works today.

Context in the ancient Near East

The major ancient Near Eastern cultures – the Babylonians, the Egyptians, and the Hittites – all preserved their own traditions about creation. In some cases, notably the eighteenth-century BC Atrahasis Epic, there is a similar sequence of presentations as in Genesis 1 – 11. The creation is followed by a flood with some intervening references of king lists, not unlike the genealogies. There is also a similarity of perspective in all the accounts as well as that of Genesis. The perspective is that of someone standing on the earth so that the sky is a great dome in which the sun, moon and planets move about in patterns. Further, the deep waters beneath the sea have an uncontrollable power that is more feared than anything. They can flood the land and destroy people and their own creations. However, there are more distinctions in

---

4. For this and other aspects of patterning in the first two chapters, see
   Richard S. Hess, 'Genesis 1–2 in Its Literary Context', *Tyndale Bulletin* 41
   (1990), pp. 143–153.

form and content than similarities between the creation account
of Genesis 1:1 – 2:4 and the many ancient Near Eastern stories.
Only Genesis has an emphasis on seven days. Only in the Genesis
account is there a clear sequence of ordering the world and then
filling it with life. The Genesis account alone describes how the
plants and animals have the power within themselves to repro-
duce. Only in the Genesis account is the image of God applied to
all humanity and the Sabbath a day of resting. Above all, the major
difference between Genesis and every account of creation outside
the Bible is that only Genesis describes one God acting alone
without reference to or acknowledgement of other deities.

Israel was part of a culture of West Semitic-speaking peoples
in the Western Levant. Among these groups, only the biblical
creation accounts are preserved. Nevertheless, there are also
conceptual distinctions between the Israelites and the surrounding nations of Canaan and the larger West Semitic context. For
example, in the Baal myth from the city of Ugarit, situated along
the coast of modern Syria, the sea is a deity. Sea is defeated by
Baal. In Genesis 1:2 the waters of the sea are mentioned and the
sea itself appears in verses 21, 26, and 28. However, it is nowhere
divine. The God of Israel does not fight the sea but creates and
controls it.

In the Canaanite and other West Semitic cultures, the fruitful-
ness of the land depends on the proper worship of deities who
provide fertility. Specific rituals are enacted and words pro-
nounced. This is not the case in the Genesis account where the
power of reproduction is inherent within the plants and animals
themselves. They have their seed in them and are capable of reproducing according to their kinds. Although the God of Israel does
give and withhold fertility in response to the nation's loyalty or dis-
loyalty, these are ethical and theological concerns, not ceremonial
ones (cf. Deut. 28).

In the West Semitic world, the sun, moon and stars were considered divine. The sun and moon were regarded as important
deities. In the land of Israel, when it was controlled by Canaanites,
the names of some of the places reflect this. The sun was named
Shemesh, and Beth Shemesh (literally 'house of the Sun', Josh.
15:10) was at some point a place of worship for the sun god.

Yerach was the name of the lunar deity. This name occurs in the famous site of Jericho which must have been a centre for moon worship. Genesis 1 does not mention the sun and moon by name. It only refers to them as the greater and lesser lights.[5] The absence of the proper names for the sun and moon implies a depersonification of these bodies. They are objects created by God and not intended for worship.

Finally, as already been noted, the beliefs that God's image resides in all people and that the Sabbath provides rest for God and all creation, are unique. This makes it all the more important to consider their purpose in the biblical narrative.

The creation summarized

The first verse of the Bible reads, 'In the beginning God created the heavens and the earth.'[6] The first word, translated in English as 'In the beginning', is probably a prepositional phrase, as in Isaiah 46:10, '. . . who tells the end from the beginning.'[7] Thus the term should be translated as a simple prepositional phrase and not a larger dependent clause, as some have argued.

The verb 'created' (Heb. *bārā'*) occurs fifty-four times in the Old Testament. It can be used interchangeably with the verbs *'āśâ* 'made, did', and *yāṣar* 'formed'. So *'āśâ* appears elsewhere as a creative act of God in Genesis 1 while *yāṣar* occurs in Genesis 2:7, 8 and 19, also with God as the subject. However, these two verbs occur elsewhere in the Bible where various people make and form things. Given the parallel usage with *bārā'* it is difficult to argue that the verb must refer to creation out of nothing. Nevertheless,

---

5. A similar term is used for the sun in one myth from the West Semitic city of Ugarit. However, this term occurs in a text that also identifies the sun by its name.

6. Bible translations are the author's.

7. The same object appears in both texts (Genesis and Isaiah) but with a different preposition. Nevertheless, Isaiah is the closest biblical Hebrew parallel to the expression in Genesis.

only God is the subject of *bārā'*. So this may refer to a distinct act of God and remains open to a possible understanding of creation out of nothing. When taken in conjunction with texts such as Isaiah 40 – 45, not to mention Colossians 1:16, this is a reasonable and coherent understanding of creation as taught in Scripture.

God here is called Elohim. This term is used of other gods in other contexts. In Genesis 1 it ascribes divine authority and power to the deity and so defines God as the creator and sovereign over the cosmos. This contrasts with the second creation story of Genesis 2:4–25. Here God is designated as Yahweh Elohim. This applies the personal name of God, Yahweh, and is appropriate for an account that emphasizes the personal relationship between God and the man and woman. Finally, the expression, the heavens and the earth, functions as a merism that includes everything from heaven above to the earth beneath.

Genesis 1:1 appears as a summary statement at the beginning of the creation account. In this manner it resembles Genesis 5:1, 'This is the genealogy of Adam' and 11:10 'This is the genealogy of Shem'. Summary statements commonly appear at the beginning of narratives in Hebrew and express an overview of what will follow. Genesis 1:1 should be understood in this manner. It could even be called a title. It does not describe an initial event followed chronologically by the events of verse 2.

Before creation

Genesis 1:2 may be translated:

> Now as for the earth,
> It was empty and unproductive:
> darkness over the face of the deep,
> God's Spirit hovering over the face of the waters.

The text isolates the earth and begins to describe in a poetic manner (note the repetition of ideas, characteristic of Hebrew poetry) what things were like before creation. The description of 'empty and unproductive' (Heb. *tōhû wābōhû*) also occurs in

Jeremiah 4:23 where the land is wasted and under divine judgment. This is a wilderness, an empty place without life or even the capacity for life. Compare the Septuagint that translates 'empty and unproductive' with a similar idea, 'invisible and unprepared'. 'The deep' translates Hebrew *těhôm*, the underground waters capable of great destructive force. These were the waters that emerged from the seas in the midst of violent storms. They might wreck ships but they could also flood inland and carry the greatest destructive force known in the ancient world.

However, God's Spirit is present. The word for Spirit (Heb. *rûah*) is also the word for wind, as in the Greek of the New Testament (Gk *pneuma*). This is important because God's Spirit appears at all major divine acts of creation and redemption. It may be associated with the 'breath' given to the man at creation in Genesis 2:7; but it certainly constitutes that which leaves humanity as it perishes in the great flood in Genesis 7:15. God's Spirit is present to give life to Israel at its birth in the Red Sea, even as it justly destroys the enemy that would prevent the birth of this nation (Exod. 15:8, 10). This parallel is especially important because in Genesis 1 the creation occurs in the context of waters. God's Spirit appears again to restore Israel at its new birth and once more to bring justice to other nations (Isa. 42:1; 44:3; 61:1). Finally, the Spirit of God is present as a wind at the birth of the Church at Pentecost (Acts 2:2).

How does one describe what existed before creation? In Genesis 1:2 the parallel lines suggest poetry and thus the use of poetic imagery to describe what is otherwise impossible to so identify. The Spirit and the waters look forward to creation. God's Spirit creates the anticipation of coming life. The empty earth, the deep and the waters form symbols of potential life.

Humanity

Genesis 1:26–28 begins the account of the creation of humanity with the words: 'God said, "Let us make the human race in our image according to our likeness".' The reference to 'us' may appear puzzling. However, to the early Israelite readers it would have pointed toward the divine council, later known as the angels and other spiritual beings who appear before God, as in Job 1 – 2, Psalm 82 and Isaiah 6. Even so, the words, 'in our image', would seem surprising. There is no reference to the image of God as involving the divine court. While a sense of the social may be implied here for the image of God (suggesting the nature of people to develop relationships rather than to be alone), the text seems to describe something distinctive about God. It could be a plural of majesty but then it is odd that it does not occur elsewhere in this text.

The 'image' (*selem*) and 'likeness' (*dĕmût*) have been described by various scholars as subtle nuances of different emphases reflecting aspects of the spiritual or physical, or dominion or service. While there may be some truth in this, the discovery of both terms on a ninth/eighth-century BC statue from Tell Fekheriyeh, a site in Northern Syria, suggests otherwise. The statue pictures a ruler and describes his accomplishments in an Aramaic text written on the body of the image. There is a parallel Assyrian translation written alongside the Aramaic. Both words, 'image' and 'likeness', are used to describe the statue; and both are translated by the same word in Assyrian. They clearly understood the terms as synonyms.[8] They represent stylistic or poetic variants and reflect the poetic elements we have already encountered in Genesis 1. The repetition reinforces the point on the statue and in Genesis.

Daniel 3:1 uses the same term to describe the statue erected by Nebuchadnezzar. It represents the king. Those who worship it worship the king. The same is true of other ancient kings. When they had conquered a territory and could no longer stay there, they might leave a statue or an image of themselves cut in the side of the mountain. It would represent royal authority. While humans are not intended to become statues, the image and likeness of God that they represent, according to this text in Genesis 1, is the divine authority. God wishes for humanity to continue the role

---

8. See further Richard S. Hess, 'Eden – A Well-Watered Place', *Bible Review* 7/6 (1991), pp. 28–33; idem, 'Genesis 1–2 and Recent Studies of Ancient Texts', *Science and Christian Belief* 7 (1995), pp. 141–149.

of the creator in having authority over the creatures and over the earth.

The use of *'ādām* to describe humanity in these verses is significant. As the parallelism of Genesis 1:27 demonstrates, the intent here is clearly to include both male and female. However, more is intended than a single couple. Every group of living creatures mentioned in Genesis 1 is given in the singular in the Hebrew and intended as a collective. So the singular 'bird' points to all the birds. The same is true with *'ādām*. It appears as a singular collective and refers to the whole group of humanity: all peoples. The referent or meaning of this term changes in the second chapter. In Genesis 2:7 – 4:24 *'ādām* regularly appears with the definite article and refers to 'the man' in relation to 'the woman'. In Genesis 4:25 and the following verses it appears without a definite article as a personal name, Adam. However, here in Genesis 1 *'ādām* denotes the entire species of humanity.[9]

The sense of God's image in Genesis 1:26–28 is not the filling of the earth, as this command is also given to animals that do not possess the divine image (e.g., Gen. 1:22). Instead, it is rulership and dominion over the earth that are described twice in these verses. The verbs, 'to rule' (Heb. *rādâ*) and 'to exercise dominion' (Heb. *kābaš*), have been understood in a variety of ways. However, the best way to understand them is within the canonical context of Genesis 1, by looking at what the man does in chapter 2. In Genesis 2:15, the man worked and took care of the garden of Eden so that it would fulfil its purpose and bear fruit. In Genesis 2:19–20 the man named the animals, discerning their purpose and function. He thus continued God's work of making the land and its vegetation for food; and of creating different kinds of animals and recognizing the distinctiveness of each one. Thus the man and the woman continued the divine act of creation. With the development of human society, this would manifest itself in various forms of culture and art. Despite

---

9. See Richard S. Hess, 'Splitting the Adam: The Usage of *'ADAM* in Genesis i-v', in J. A. Emerton (ed.), *Studies in the Pentateuch* (Supplements to *Vetus Testamentum* XLI; Leiden: Brill, 1990), pp. 1–15.

human failure (Gen. 3:1–19; 4:1–24; 6:1–13; 11:1–9), God sought to teach people how to reflect the divine image. Therefore, one family and a people were chosen. From Genesis 12 to the end of the Old Testament, the story describes how they received detailed instruction on the manner in which to reflect that image before the world and thus to be a kingdom of priests (Exod. 19:6). Their failures and successes are recorded, as well as the further instruction of the prophets and wisdom literature. For Christians, Jesus Christ comes as the true image of God (2 Cor. 4:4; Col. 1:15). His proclamation of the kingdom of God is the proclamation of that image. The challenge is passed on to the church, which continues to express God's image in the service and transformation of the world until today.

The text of Genesis contains a great deal of wordplay. Thus humanity, Hebrew *'ādām,* is created from the ground, Hebrew *'ădāmâ,* and will return to it in death (Gen. 2:7; 3:19). The *'ādām* works at the *'ădāmâ* and is in charge of the Garden. He enjoys harmony with the soil and it responds to him just as creation responded to the Creator. The woman is created equally from the side of the man (Gen. 2:21–22). In Hebrew, the *-āh* (*-â*) suffix is the characteristic feminine ending. However, the man cannot use the already taken wordplay *'ādām/'ădāmâ* (man/ground), but uses another Hebrew word pair, *'îš/'iššâ* (man/woman), to demonstrate the harmony between the two in Genesis 2:23. The following verse should not be taken to describe the establishment of a matriarchal society. A man shall leave his parents and join to his wife so as to restore what was separated when the woman was created from the man.

Both Adam and Eve have names that define unique aspects of their roles. We have already seen how Adam is the Hebrew *'ādām* and plays on the word for the ground (*'ădāmâ*) that he works. He is 'the man of the Garden', a title that can refer to one who is governor over a region; in this case it is Eden. The man discerns the unique role of the woman when he names her Eve (Hebrew *ḥawwâ*) in Genesis 3:20. This form of a noun is often used of occupations. The Hebrew root means 'to live, be alive'. In this form it carries that sense, 'to give life'. Thus Eve is 'life giver', a name describing her unique role in light of Genesis 3:16.

Summary

How can we summarize the implications of Genesis 1:1 – 2:4?

First, creation is cosmological in Genesis 1 where God is described as Elohim and sovereign creator God of all. In Genesis 2:4–22 creation is anthropological as Yahweh Elohim establishes a personal relationship with the man and then the woman, providing their home, food, and responsibilities.

Second, the seven days of creation are logical rather than chronological. The days correspond to the generations of the later genealogies in Genesis. This is why they are also called *tôlĕdôt*. Thus the God of creation is the same God who works in each generation of humanity up to the present.

Third, creation is not primarily ontological but concerned with life. Perhaps the most important theological purpose of Genesis 1 is the creation of life. God creates the contexts for life in the first three days and then fills this background with teeming abundant life in days four to six.

Fourth, creation climaxes on the seventh day as the day of God's resting. Thus rest is built into the order of creation as the Sabbath will later recall (Deut. 5:12–15). All creation moves forward to enjoy a final great Sabbath rest at the end of time (cf. Heb. 4:1–11).

Fifth and finally, creation was meant to be led and guided by *'ādām* who is created in God's image as male and female. Humanity is given stewardship over all creation. The image is never destroyed, despite sin and violence. Rather, according to the New Testament the image is perfected in Jesus Christ. And that image continues in humanity today as a call to reflect God's will and kingdom through the ongoing work of serving humanity and of transforming culture according to the divine will.

5. ORIGINAL SIN AND THE FALL: DEFINITIONS AND A PROPOSAL

T. A. Noble

The doctrine of original sin and the doctrine of the Fall are inextricably linked in historic Christianity. The doctrine of original sin is about the human condition; 'the Fall' is the term traditionally employed for human disobedience and its consequences as recounted in the narrative of Genesis 3 and given its Christian interpretation by Paul, particularly in chapter 5 of his letter to the Romans. A difficulty with the doctrine of original sin is that it is rather a complex concept. The major problem with the doctrine of the Fall arising in the modern era is how to cope with the difficulty of assigning it a place in history or pre-history, which Pauline doctrine seems to require. The alternative, taken by many in the light of the story of human origins established by modern science, is to reinterpret it and dispense with the idea that the Fall was an event. But in addition to those problems, there is the further difficulty that both doctrines seem to be highly paradoxical. Humanity, the highest creature of the world which God created and, in Genesis 1, pronounces 'very good', inexplicably disbelieves and disobeys the Creator. That is paradoxical enough. But then as a result, human beings are wilfully blind: we cannot see because we will not, and we will not because we cannot. That is a further paradox. We are still in some sense free, yet not free; able to please God (as Abel apparently did), yet not able to believe, obey and repair the breach; wilfully blind in a way which is blameworthy, yet incapable of seeing, knowing and acknowledging God as we ought; enslaved to our own wilfulness. We will not believe and obey because we cannot, and we cannot because we will not.

Given that bundle of problems and paradoxes, this chapter will attempt to do only two things. First, since the concept of original sin is much more complex than is often realized, we shall attempt conceptual clarification by trying to identify its different facets. This will not be a full exercise in historical theology since we shall make little attempt here to identify those who first delineated or subsequently held to the various facets, far less to document who held what down through the centuries.[1] We shall confine ourselves largely to logical clarification. The hope is that by distinguishing what may be thought of either as different usages of the term 'original sin', or as distinguishable but interconnected facets of the concept, we may be better able to clarify discussion by avoiding conceptual confusion. This analysis may be seen as a useful preliminary to the task of the biblical or historical theologian in comparing what different biblical writers and Christian theologians actually say.[2]

The second half of the paper turns more specifically to the doctrine of the Fall and is an attempt at framing a theological proposal about how the Fall should be regarded. This is more of a constructive attempt at theology, without claiming to present a fully developed doctrine. It has in view the problem of relating the biblical narrative of the Fall as it has been interpreted in historic Christianity to the narrative given by modern science and history,

---

1. The classic attempt to do that comprehensively was N. P. Williams, *The Ideas of the Fall and Original Sin* (London: Longmans, 1927), the Bampton Lectures for 1924.

2. The material for this first half of the chapter is drawn from a conference paper given in 2000 and circulated privately in the proceedings of the conference, published as 'Prolegomena for a Conference on Original Sin', in *European Explorations in Christian Holiness* 2 (2001), pp. 6–18.

but it does not address that question directly. Rather it is concerned with how the doctrine of the Fall should be regarded as a matter of Christian doctrine. It cannot be stressed too much that that is a necessary preliminary to comparing the two 'stories'. The Christian narrative of the Fall must not and cannot be formulated on the grounds of *both* revelation *and* contemporary science and history. It must be formulated within the integrity of Christian theology, that is to say, on the ground of revelation. But it may be formulated on that ground in such a way that leaves open the possibility of some kind of correlation of the biblical story and the scientific story. That is a subsequent task, and to try to conflate the two is to muddle two different methodologies, that of theological science and that of natural science. That is the kind of muddled thinking which treats the *doctrine* of creation as if it were a *scientific theory*. Rather the attempt here will be to float a theological proposal for consideration, a view of the beginning in the light of the end, that is, looking at the Fall in the light of New Testament eschatology.

The concept of 'original sin': ten facets

We begin then with the question which should be asked before we attempt any examination of the doctrine of original sin in biblical, historical or contemporary theology: *what* are we actually looking for in the Old Testament, in the literature of Judaism, in the New Testament, in Irenaeus, Augustine, the Reformers, Barth or Pannenberg, when we look for a doctrine of 'original sin'? This is not the dogmatic question: how *ought* the doctrine of original sin to be formulated? The question here is the prior question: *how has it actually been formulated*? If we are not going to be talking at cross purposes when investigating the history of the doctrine or coming to some theological assessment and formulation of it, we need some consistent though preliminary idea of what we are looking for. The *concept* is of course to a large degree Augustinian, but not entirely. Some of the facets precede Augustine and have been held universally in the Church.

The best way to define such a 'pre-understanding' of the concept is to list the different facets. They are not totally discrete but all interconnect, and so are best described as 'facets'. Laying them out in this way may help us to see what a complex concept this is. At least ten connected facets may be discerned. They are rarely (if ever) all present in any one document, and since writers tend to slide from one to another, this can confuse the discussion. Certainly some facets imply others, but we must not jump to the conclusion that because one is present others are implied in any one writer. Nor must we assume that a doctrine of original sin must include them all. Because they interconnect in a complex way, it is not possible to put them in a completely linear arrangement, but the following order is probably as good as any.

1. Universal sin

The first facet, universal sin, strictly speaking falls short of the concept of 'original sin', but sometimes this is all that is meant: that 'all have sinned and fall short of the glory of God' (Rom. 3:23[3]). While this concept is 'universal', it is also individualistic, and that is how Pelagius seems to have understood it, denying that Adam and Eve passed on a state of sinfulness or mortality to their descendants. Whilst he did not claim that there were any human beings who had lived sinlessly throughout the whole of their lives, he nonetheless pointed to those in Scripture who attained a state of sinlessness.[4] For him, sin resulted from the influences of sinful human families and communities, from nurture, not nature. Since the doctrine of the sinfulness of humanity was for him an assertion that all individuals were sinful, like all inductive conclusions it was open to denial by finding exceptions.

2. Fallenness

Fallenness is the idea of being in a fallen state or condition as a result of the event called 'the Fall', and for Augustinian Western Christianity, the Fall resulted in original sin, and therefore to be

---

3. All Bible quotations in this chapter are NRSV.
4. Augustine quotes the list in 'On Nature and Grace', 42 *NPNF*, 1st series, vol. 5, p. 135. For a summary of the teaching of Pelagius, see J. N. D. Kelly, *Early Christian Doctrines* (London: Black, [4]1968).

'fallen' is primarily to be sinful.[5] This term is therefore often
taken in the West to mean 'being subject to original sin'. In the
Greek Fathers, however, the focus is more on the ontological
results of the Fall. According to this idea we are mortal, subject
to *phthora*, usually translated 'corruption'.[6] Unfortunately that
English word is ambiguous, since it may mean either physical or
moral corruption. It is better to translate *phthora* as 'decay', since
what is primarily in mind is not moral corruption or sinfulness,
but the ontological state of being subject to decay, disease, disintegration and death. It is 'physical' corruption, meaning the decay
of our human *physis* (nature). In the thought of the Greek Fathers
this goes together with the belief that the Son of God assumed our
fallen humanity (meaning by that our *mortal* humanity), but, since
he sanctified our humanity in the very taking it, for them this did
not compromise the sinlessness of Christ's human nature. Yet his
taking of our mortal, decaying, dying humanity was vital to them,
for (as Gregory of Nazianzus famously put it), 'The unassumed
is the unhealed.'[7] Unless he took 'flesh', *our* common, corporate,
mortal humanity, then the victory of the resurrection means
nothing for us mortals. Unless he took it and sanctified it in his
own Person by the power of the Holy Spirit, then we cannot be
holy either here or hereafter.

---

5. An introduction to Augustine's doctrine of original sin will be found in
   Kelly, *Doctrines*, pp. 361–366, a fuller account in Lecture 5 in Williams,
   Ideas of the Fall, pp. 315–390, and a more recent explanation in Paul Rigby,
   'Original Sin', in Allan D. Fitzgerald (ed.), *Augustine through the Ages: An
   Encyclopaedia* (Grand Rapids: Eerdmans, 1999), pp. 607–614.
6. This is the word group used by Paul in Rom. 8:21 and 1 Cor. 15:50–54,
   and by Athanasius in 'On the Incarnation', *NPNF*, 2nd series, vol. 4 (and
   also in several other editions).
7. Gregory of Nazianzus, Epistle 101 (*NPNF*, 2nd series, vol. 7), p. 438.
   For Athanasius' classic exposition of this doctrine, see 'Incarnation',
   pp. 31–67. Nazianzen and Athanasius are representative here of the
   Fathers who formulated the orthodox doctrine of Christ, but not all
   modern theologians agree. See, for example, Donald Macleod, *The Person
   of Christ* (Leicester: IVP, 1998), pp. 224ff.

Here we need to note in passing that this second facet of the meaning of the concept of original sin connects it directly to the concept of 'the Fall'. Some have tried to cut out the idea of the Fall as a primeval event and yet retain the concept of 'fallenness'. That debate introduces vast and methodologically complicated questions of hermeneutics, theology, and the relationship of revelation to history and to science. Unfortunately these difficult questions are too often answered superficially on both sides of the debate by confusing the methodologies of theology and natural science, each of which is valid within its own horizons at its own level of understanding. We cannot deal with all the questions exhaustively here, but the proposal in the second half of the chapter will attempt to suggest a direction of thinking which could be fruitfully developed.

3. The original act of sin

A third facet of the meaning of the concept is 'the original act of sin'. In the narrative of Genesis 3, the eating of the fruit of the tree of the knowledge of good and evil was *the* original sin, the sin from which all sin originates. This usage may be more typically Eastern,[8] for the phrase *peccatum originale* appears to have been rarely if ever used in this way in the West. But this points once again to the connection between the concept of original sin and the concept of the Fall as a primeval event. The term 'the Fall' has been used since the early centuries to include both this original act of sin and the consequences, banishment and mortality, which followed. But although this initial act is an inherent part of the concept, the phrase 'original sin' has been used to refer primarily (if not exclusively) to the next two facets.

4. Original guilt

Augustine taught that we all sinned in Adam and therefore shared in the *reatus*, the legal guilt for his sin.[9] This was connected with

---

8. This is the view of Ian McFarland, in 'The Fall and Sin', in J. Webster, K. Tanner and I. Torrance (eds.) *The Oxford Handbook of Systematic Theology* (Oxford: OUP, 2007), pp. 140–159.

9. *Enchiridion*, 26, 27 (*NPNF*, 1st series, vol. 3), pp. 237–276; see p. 246.

his understanding of Romans 5:12 from the Old Latin as 'one man . . . in whom (*in quo*) all sinned'. This original guilt was remitted, however, in baptism. This Augustinian legacy continued in the post-Reformation Church of England, so that Wesley (for example) could refer to his 'original sin' (in this sense of the term) being washed away in baptism.[10] The idea of inherited guilt has often been puzzling, not to say immoral, for individualistic Western thought.

5. Original sin as a vitium or disease

Here we come to the meaning of the term which dominates contemporary usage. 'Original sin' is primarily understood today to mean, not so much a legal sharing in the guilt of Adam, but a kind of inherited disease. This is presumably a metaphor, but when such metaphors become the chief way of speaking of anything, they tend to become dead metaphors, that is to say, they tend to be taken almost literally. This 'disease' is said to be 'inborn' or 'inbred' and is sometimes referred to as our 'sinful nature', that is, a diseased condition with which we are born (*natus*). It is in this meaning of the term that 'original sin' is affirmed by all orthodox Catholic and Protestant theologians. Article 9 of the Anglican Thirty-Nine Articles refers to it as 'the fault and corruption of the nature of every man . . . whereby man is very far gone from original righteousness, and is of his own nature inclined to evil'. It is an 'infection of nature' and it remains even 'in them that are regenerated'. This is the facet of the concept which Wesley defended in his sermon, 'Original Sin'[11] on Genesis 6:5 and in his treatise on original sin in response to the deist, John Taylor of Norwich.[12]

But some confusion arises here from the way we use the term 'nature'. When we speak of the 'sinful nature', do we mean that

---

10. See Wesley's *Journal* for 24th May 1738.
11. John Wesley, 'Original Sin', Sermon 44, *Works*, vol. 2 (Nashville: Abingdon, 1985), pp. 170–185.
12. John Wesley, 'The Doctrine of Original Sin', *Works*, vol. 9 (Kansas City: Nazarene Publishing House, n.d.), pp. 191–464. This treatise has not yet been published in the new Abingdon critical edition.

original sin in this sense is a kind of disease or deficiency 'in' our human nature? Or do we mean that the nature itself is so warped and twisted that it has become the source of our sinning? The close identification of 'original sin' and 'the sinful nature' may seem to suggest the latter, but the Lutheran Formula of Concord makes a point of differentiating between them.[13] The confusion surrounding the word 'nature' was surely worse confounded when the translators of the NIV took it upon themselves not to *translate* the word *sarx* (which strictly speaking means 'flesh'), but to *paraphrase* it as 'sinful nature' in certain passages.[14] The phrase 'sinful nature' (found nowhere in the Greek New Testament) surely encourages close identification of human nature with original sin. Human nature is indeed sinful (we must reject Pelagius for Augustine), but it is not inherently evil since it was created good, and it is certainly not to be *identified with* original sin. Such an identification would land us in the heretical ditches on the other side of the narrow way, either Manichaeism or Gnosticism of some kind.

Then there is the further question of what exactly we mean by 'nature'. It has sometimes been said that those 'born again' have a new nature (from *natus*, born), but that the old sinful nature does not die. When that is taken literally we have the very confusing idea of two 'natures' within the regenerate person, two entities, as it were.

We also need to relate this to the way the word 'depravity' has traditionally been used. It is probably best not to distinguish 'depravity' as a distinct facet of the concept of original sin, because it is largely synonymous with the metaphor of original sin as a 'disease'. There is perhaps a slight difference in that our 'nature' is said to be 'depraved' as a *result* of this disease of sin. The 'sinful nature', or the fact that our nature is in fact sinful, or our being

---

13. See Article 1 of the Formula of Concord, in Philip Schaff (ed.), *The Creeds of Christendom*, vol. 3 (Grand Rapids: Baker, 1983), pp. 97f.

14. This choice was no doubt in accordance with their adherence to Augustinian and Reformation orthodoxy in their doctrine of sin, but this kind of loose translation is surely too much in danger of reading the translator's theological interpretation into the text.

'depraved', is the *result* of the disease rather than the disease itself. But it is not clear how far such a fine distinction is necessary in analyzing the facets. Possibly, however, researches in the history of theology would suggest that it would prove helpful to list this separately as another facet, bringing the total to eleven. (Ten seems tidier!) The phrase '*total* depravity' is also part of Augustinian anthropology, and obviously another way of expressing original sin as a disease (or its result).

6. Hereditary sinfulness

The sixth facet, hereditary sinfulness, is very difficult to separate from the last two. Indeed we have already referred to (4), original guilt, as 'inherited'. But it can be *logically* separated certainly from (5), original sin as *vitium* or disease. Not all diseases are inherited, and therefore (5) does not logically entail (6). It may be helpful therefore in this analytical task to distinguish the idea of heredity as a distinct facet of the concept. It has always *in fact* gone with (5) (as is seen if we complete the quotation from Article 9 of the Thirty-Nine Articles, 'every man, that naturally is engendered of the offspring of Adam'), but it would be possible to separate them in logic. When we do, we can see that the concept of heredity is one of the major problems for modern Western thinking, and indeed poses problems for both (4) and (5).[15]

The problem for (4) is the ethical problem: how can guilt be inherited? As for (5), we are familiar with inherited disease, but the problem here is the mechanism. We can see how a physical disease can be inherited, but this is presumably not a physical disease. What on earth then is the mechanism for passing on a spiritual or moral disease? The outcome of such a line of questioning is to make it clear that Augustine's language of a *vitium* or disease must be understood as metaphorical. Part of our problem here may be that we are taking models too literally and are therefore bound to find them inconsistent.

---

15. Barth criticized the German term for original sin, *Erbsünde*, since it literally means 'hereditary sin', and proposed the term *Ursünde*, meaning 'sin at the source or origin' (*CD*, IV/1, pp. 500f.).

7. An inner disposition, tendency or 'bent toward sinning'

At the root of the seventh facet, the disposition, tendency or bent to sinning is Augustine's term *concupiscentia*, but some explanation of this term is called for to avoid confusion. *Concupiscentia* gives us our English word, 'concupiscence', but the latter is more restricted in meaning. 'Concupiscence' means quite specifically 'sexual desire', but the Latin word has a broader meaning. The verb *concupisco* simply means 'to desire ardently, to covet'. The root of the word is *cupido*, from which also comes the noun *cupiditas*, an eager desire, from which we get the English word 'cupidity', greed or avarice. Although the sexual connotations are prominent therefore in the Latin words (we all know about Cupid), the word is not restricted to that by any means. *Concupiscentia* may therefore be interpreted as 'self-centred desire'. Augustine's model of human motivation is that our *amor* (love, affection) is either directed to God (in which case it is *caritas*) or else it is directed to the creaturely realm (in which case it is *concupiscentia* or *cupiditas*).[16]

Whereas *vitium* is a metaphor for sinfulness as a disease, *concupiscentia* is part of a psychological analysis of this condition in terms of human motivation. It is this facet of the concept of original sin which Wesley identified with Paul's phrase in Romans 8:5–7, the *phronēma tēs sarkos*, 'the mind that is set on the flesh'.[17] This then is the facet of the concept which is most obviously connected with Wesley's understanding of 'perfect love' or 'purity of heart' as the victory of single-minded *caritas* (whole-hearted love for God) over what we may paraphrase as 'the self-centred mind-set', which we may identify with Augustine's concept of *concupiscentia*.

8. The propagation of sin through sexual desire

This eighth facet of the Augustinian concept of 'original sin' probably partly explains why the meaning of the English word

---

16. Among numerous passages, see *In Ps.* XXXI (*NPNF*, vol. 8); *De doctrina Christiana*, III, x, 15–16; *De Trinitate*, IX, 7–8, 13 (*NPNF*, vol. 3, pp. 130f.).
17. See for example, Sermon 13, 'On Sin in Believers', IV.7, *Works*, vol. 1 (Nashville: Abingdon, 1984), pp. 317–334; or Sermon 43, 'The Scripture Way of Salvation', III.6, *Works*, vol. 2, pp. 155–169.

'concupiscence' has narrowed to 'sexual desire'. For although the Latin term had a wider meaning, Augustine, as part of his Roman heritage, associated sanctity with chastity, and sin with sexuality, and so tended to see sexual desire at the heart of all our wrong desires.[18] Specifically, he devised an explanation of the passing on the *vitium* which he repeated ad nauseam. The mechanism of inheritance, he claimed, was in the lust of the father which preceded every human birth. This gave him, of course, a nice neat explanation of the virginal conception of Jesus as safeguarding his sinlessness, but at the cost of casting a slur and an insult on sexual relations within marriage which, according to Scripture, God ordained and blesses.[19]

There are two problems with this theory of Augustine. First, as part of his Roman inheritance it has no basis in the positive Hebrew evaluation of human sexuality which is to be expressed in marriage. His theory of the transmission of original sin through lust is without foundation in the biblical literature, and must be dismissed as bizarre. Augustine's twisted evaluation of human sexuality is a distortion for which we are now paying a high price in the Church's inability to cope with the wild reaction against Augustinian sexual repression which surged through twentieth-century literature and culture. Secondly, it seems to sit oddly with the idea that our *nature* is sinful. If it is our *nature* which is sinful, the alleged lust of every father is irrelevant, for congenital sin would be inherited from mothers, who also share in the diseased, sinful human nature. (It was that problem, of course, which gave the logic underlying the development of the medieval Catholic doctrine of the immaculate conception of Mary.)

---

18. Cf. Gerald Bray's argument that Tertullian derives the equation of sanctity with chastity from the old Roman religion in Gerald L. Bray, *Holiness and the Will of God: Perspectives on the Theology of Tertullian* (London: Marshall and Atlanta: John Knox Press, 1979).

19. For the way in which Augustine linked this with the doctrine of the virgin birth (an interpretation widely held in the West) see *On the Trinity* 13, ch. 18 (*NPNF*, 1st series, vol. 3, p. 180).

9. The flesh

The eighth facet brings us to a term which is actually biblical! But because it has been interpreted so often through Augustinian spectacles, it has taken on a meaning closely connected with the full Augustinian concept of original sin. At the risk of over-simplification, we need to distinguish four usages of *sarx* in the biblical literature, each a development of the one before:

1. *sarx* meaning the physical flesh, or the individual human being viewed from the perspective of physical existence; this physical flesh is weak and mortal, but not evil;
2. *sarx* meaning 'all flesh', that is, the human race in its corporate solidarity, the humanity which is common to all the race; human nature, that which the Word assumed, considered corporately; humanity as weak and mortal and sinful, but not inherently evil;
3. *sarx* as that in which we put our trust, a peculiarly Pauline usage from which he develops his concept of the *phronēma sarkos*, the mind 'set on the flesh' (NRSV);
4. *sarx* as a power within which is in conflict with the Spirit – a peculiarly Pauline concept again.[20]

Number (4) appears in Galatians 5, chronologically before (3), but (3) seems to be the missing link, the conceptual bridge from (2) to (4) which makes it clear that (4) is not to be interpreted in a gnostic way. The power of the flesh within does not mean that the 'flesh' is inherently evil, but that the power we are enslaved to is our own self-centredness, the disposition to live for merely human goals and values.[21]

It is in this context that we must interpret the phrase 'desires of the flesh' (*epithymiai sarkos*), to make it clear that, while the phrase is used pejoratively in Scripture, these desires are sinful because

---

20. Cf. E. Schweitzer's article on *sarx* in Kittel's *Theological Dictionary of the New Testament* (Grand Rapids: Wm. B. Eerdmans Publishing, 1964), and Hans Walter Wolff, *Anthropology of the Old Testament* (London: SCM, 1974).
21. Cf. Matt Jenson, *The Gravity of Sin: Augustine, Luther and Barth on* homo incurvatus in se (Edinburgh: T.& T. Clark, 2007).

they are *misdirected* and *out of control*. The doctrine of creation makes
it clear that the basic physiological desires created by God are not
evil in themselves as the Reformation traditions may sometimes
seem to suggest.[22] At the same time, the holistic thinking of Old
Testament anthropology makes it clear that they are not unaffected
by human sinfulness since the Fall, and that their 'inordinate' state
is part of human 'fallenness'.

10. Corporate sin

Finally we come to a concept too seldom developed in our individualistic European culture. But this is surely a facet of original
sin which holds out the best hope for an imaginative and creative
development which can make it speak to contemporary issues.
We must not abandon the perceptive Augustinian analysis of the
psychology of human motivation which deepens the concept
already in the Greek Fathers of Christian 'perfection' or maturity. In the West, this model of human motivation lies behind the
development of the concept of 'purity of heart' or 'perfection
in love' which we find in Bernard, Aquinas and Wesley. But this
psychological analysis needs to be complemented by a deeper
understanding of original sin as corporate. If the focus were here,
it would shift the focus from the problematic concept of heredity,
always conceived of individualistically. The conundrum of how we
each individually inherit Adam's sin has allowed our attention to be
diverted from the understanding of *humanity's corporate solidarity in
sinfulness*. We may have to work at the business of communicating
this Old Testament concept of corporate solidarity to our individualistic European culture, but at least the much-heralded tide
of (so-called) 'postmodernism' is supposed to be moving attention
from the individual to the community. And it is certainly easier to
communicate the idea of corporate responsibility and corporate

---

22. For example, Calvin, *Institutes*, 3:3: 10–12: 'there is always sin in the saints
until they are freed from their mortal frame, because depraved concupiscence resides in their flesh', 'all human desires are evil . . .'. Calvin does
attempt (somewhat inconsistently) to make the same distinction between
our desires as created and our desires as fallen.

guilt than to defend the idea of hereditary guilt. Corporate sinfulness is also at the heart of Walter Wink's profound analysis of the powers of evil as the product of the 'domination system' of corporate human society.[23]

Corporate sin in Adam also connects of course, as Paul shows us, with the idea of our corporate solidarity in Christ, the Last Adam. In fact our understanding of corporate sin is, properly speaking, a *consequence* of our understanding of corporate salvation in Christ.

The quick review of these ten facets then by no means answers all the questions, but this kind of analysis can surely help us in the more constructive task of crafting a more concise and coherent doctrine of original sin.

The doctrine of the Fall: a proposal

Turning secondly to the doctrine of the Fall, we will now attempt to sketch a dogmatic approach under three headings:

* alienation, dealing with the event of the Fall,
* death,
* sin.

Once again it needs to be emphasized that this is an 'essay' in the technical sense of that word. That is to say that it is an 'attempt', an initial sketch, a proposal for discussion rather than a fully documented scholarly paper, but it does attempt to focus on what is *theologically* essential to a doctrine of the Fall. That means that we must not attempt to articulate a doctrine of the Fall as a foundation for the gospel, arguing from Adam to Christ: rather we must

---

23. Walter Wink, *Naming the Powers* (Minneapolis: Augsburg Fortress, 1984), *Unmasking the Powers* (Minneapolis: Augsburg Fortress, 1986), *Engaging the Powers* (Minneapolis: Augsburg Fortress, 1992). For my own assessment, see T. A. Noble, 'The Spirit World: A Theological Approach', in A. N. S. Lane (ed.), *The Unseen World* (Grand Rapids: Baker, 1996), pp. 185–223.

see the doctrine of the Fall as a necessary implication of the gospel of salvation, arguing from Christ to Adam. A *Christian* doctrine of the Fall cannot therefore be simply extrapolated from Genesis, but must be articulated (as indeed it was historically) as Genesis is understood in the light of the gospel, that is, in the light of the New Testament.

Alienation

The first point to make is that humanity is alienated from God: hostility disrupts the relationship. In the historic Christian understanding of both Eastern and Western Christian theology, that is because of an *event*, the Fall. Christian theology is committed then to two affirmations.

The Fall is at its heart a spiritual and ethical event

According to the narrative of Genesis 3, humanity (*Adam*, the man, with *Eve*, the mother of all living) chose not to trust the word of God and so was *unfaithful*. That was the spiritual event, 'spiritual' in the sense of 'relational': it was the breaking of a relationship between God and humanity. The ethical consequence of that spiritual-relational break was Adam's disobedience. As a free agent, he *rebelled* against God. By saying this, we opt for the Christian doctrine of the Fall and thus reject the historic metaphysical alternatives, monism (as in Hinduism) and dualism (as in the Persian religions). The doctrine of the Fall (we must understand), is not an *explanation* of evil: it is the only choice open to us in order to reject these metaphysical *explanations*. Indeed, the doctrine of the Fall *cannot* be an explanation, for evil is inexplicable by definition for Christians. It is the chaos in God's cosmos: it opposes chaos and disorder to God's rational structure and order. It is the 'anti-logos' to God's Logos. Since rational explanation arises out of rational structure and order, chaos is by definition irrational and inexplicable. It is as darkness to light (as both Johannine and Pauline theology see it); that is, as negative to positive. We can no more have a Christian demonology to complement our theology than we may have a physics of darkness to complement our physics of light.

Instead we must opt for this: that God's good creatures, in an inexplicable, irrational act of madness and wilful folly, were *unfaithful* to God's word, sought their own glory, and *disobeyed* and *rebelled* against the Creator. This paradoxical doctrine embedded in the narrative of Genesis 3 is the only way to escape metaphysical monism or dualism.[24] Both of those are unacceptable to Christian faith, because both locate the origin of evil *beyond the created realm* (which is the realm of time) and therefore *within* the Uncreated. Monism locates the origin of evil within the One God; dualism postulates an uncreated principle of evil, a rival god equal to God in eternity and power, his eternal opposite. Since we must exclude both of these alternatives, the paradoxical doctrine of the Fall is therefore a necessary part of Christian theology. That means that we should not think of the doctrine of the Fall as a form of theodicy, an explanation of sin and evil or an attempt to justify God. It does not 'explain' at all! As a Christian doctrine, it is not part of apologetics: it is a necessary part of Christian dogmatics. It asserts the irrationality and absurdity of evil as that which God did not intend and did not create. God has not given us an intellectual explanation of evil: instead he *came* in the person of his Son to suffer the worst that evil could do to him and to die to redeem us and all creation from its power.

The Fall is an event in time
This second affirmation which historic Christianity makes in the doctrine of the Fall is that it was an event within the created realm, that is, within time. N. P. Williams wrote: 'It is impossible to lift the Fall out of the time series without falling either into Manichaeism or unmoral monism . . . The Fall, whatever else it may have been, must have been an event in time.'[25] This is essential to the concept of the Fall as the rebellion of corporate humanity due to unbelief and pride. It must be conceived of as a single, corporate Fall in time.

---

24. Process theology is a more subtle form of dualism, since evil and suffering, while in the world, are as eternal as the world is, and will never be abolished, since the eternal process in which God 'lures' the world to its *telos* never ends.
25. Williams, *Ideas of the Fall,* Synopsis, p. xxxiii.

Oscar Cullmann was among many who have accepted that the *language* of Genesis 3 is 'saga' or 'prophetic' or even 'myth' (although that is a slippery and misleading term) but that the event it describes is temporal, that it actually happened in this world.[26] He argued that whereas we may distinguish between 'history' and 'myth', the early Christians did not. Therefore we do violence to their understanding of salvation history if, like Bultmann, we 'demythologize' the Fall and make it into a 'timeless' event. Bultmann similarly 'demythologized' the eschatological event of the *parousia*, making it into a 'timeless' event. For him as the quintessential theologian of twentieth-century modernity, the gospel was not cosmic: it was individual. What matters is my existential decision, my 'conversion', my 'crisis'. To speak of 'the Fall' is simply to say that humanity is 'fallen', that is, that we live inauthentically, tied to the dead past, not looking forward in hope and faith. The story of the Fall is therefore to be regarded as a myth, a story expressing a *timeless* truth. Similarly, the *parousia* simply speaks of the urgency of the decision that each one must make. According to Cullmann, this demythologizing did not succeed in removing the husk (a 'mythological' worldview) and leaving the kernel (justification by faith interpreted as existential decision). Rather, it distorted the New Testament gospel, which is about God's action *in history*.

To be true to the Christian gospel, therefore, we must maintain a temporal Fall even though the language used is prophetic and full of imagery (the tree of the knowledge of good and evil, as much imagery as the great white throne, the lake of fire, or the bottomless pit), and, we may not be able to date this event since it may not be open to our historical inquiries. It may be 'historical' in one sense (that it actually happened), but not historical in another sense (that it is established as having happened by inquiry according to the historical-critical method).

Sometimes attempts have been made to date the Fall, or at least

---

26. Cullmann, *Christ and Time* (London: SCM, 1951) esp. ch 6 (pp. 94–106).
See also James Orr, *The Christian View of God and the World* (Edinburgh: Andrew Elliot, 1893), pp. 212ff.

to fit Adam and the Fall into ancient history and pre-history. C.S. Lewis, for example, in *The Problem of Pain*,[27] attempted to place the Fall within the evolutionary development of the human race.

But before we even begin to speculate about some correlation between an event which is necessarily posited as an integral part of the Christian revelation and modern scientific accounts of human origins, we must first clarify the doctrine of the Fall in the light of the Christian understanding of *time*, and that has to be eschatological. In other words, the way in which Christian theology should articulate its 'protology', the doctrine of the first things, is in the light of eschatology, the doctrine of the last things.

It first became obvious with Johannes Weiss and Albert Schweitzer that eschatology was not just the future end of the biblical story, but that New Testament thought was eschatological through and through. By the mid-twentieth century, scholars such as Cullmann, Kümmel and Ladd had established that the eschatology of Jesus and of the New Testament writers was about a kingdom which had *already* come in Jesus as a hidden mystery, but which had *not yet* come in glory and power. Where first-century Jewish eschatology (as the framework of thought for most though not all Jews) thought of Israel as living in 'this present evil age', while expecting 'the age to come' when Rome would be overthrown and the kingdom of David re-established, the new Christian movement believed that Messiah had *already* come, and had *already* been raised from the dead, and had *already* sent down the Spirit in all his fullness, but that the kingly rule of God had *not yet* come in glory and power. By the mid-twentieth century, systematic theologians such as Pannenberg and Moltmann were trying to incorporate the new understanding of New Testament eschatology into Christian theology as a whole. Every doctrine had to begin from this point. This was the key in which the whole Christian symphony had to be set.

Since the structure of New Testament thinking is eschatological through and through, the consequence for Christian theology is that every doctrine must be thought through eschatologically,

---

27. 'The Fall of Man', *The Problem of Pain* (London: Geoffrey Bles, 1940), ch. 5.

and since to speak of the 'ages' is to use the terminology of *time*, eschatology must shape the way in which Christians think about time. The temporal structure we have to bear in mind then is the great division between 'this present evil age' and 'the age to come', not the Platonist division between this world below and the world above (although there is also a biblical 'below' and 'above'). This 'present evil age' is then to be understood as 'fallen time': the 'age to come' is 'redeemed time'. That may be seen to have a further implication, although here we may be influenced too by the way in which 'time' has been re-conceived in the decades since Einstein. The implication is that 'time' is not an independent self-existent entity or reality 'within' which events happen; it is not some 'thing' with ontological priority, as if the 'timeline' somehow existed first and we then plotted events upon it. Rather, just as lines of longitude and latitude on a map do not pre-exist the geographical features which are marked on the map, so time and space are not independent, autonomous *receptacles* (as in Aristotelian or Newtonian cosmology) 'within' which events happen. The measurements we make of time and space are based on real objects, real events, but are *derived from them*. For example, a year is not a pre-existent unit of measurement, it is the length of time taken by the earth to go round the sun: a day is the time it takes for the earth to revolve. In other words, these events are *prior*, our measurements are based on them. Units of time are functions of occurring and recurring events. Time is not then a pre-existent absolute, a constant 'within' which the relative events (including the birth and development of the universe) occur. It is rather ontologically dependent on the universe, a *dimension* of the universe. To say that events occur 'in' time is therefore misleading: time is measured by events. It is the events which are the basis for the way humans devise measurements of time.[28]

---

28. Behind this simplified explanation lies T. F. Torrance's distinction between a *receptacle* notion of space/time (which he traces from Aristotle, Stoicism and the Florentine Academy during the Renaissance, to Gassendi, Galileo and Newton) and a *relational* notion (which he traces through Clement and other Church Fathers, Anselm, Duns Scotus,

So for Christians, the 'age to come' will begin with the *parousia* when the kingdom of God comes in glory and power. The new measurement of time will begin with a cosmic event which will transform the cosmos in such a way that it will form the 'new creation' composed of 'the new heavens and the new earth'. This radical transformation of the cosmos to which we look forward in hope involves some kind of physical renewal of the cosmos itself beyond our ability to imagine. In some way, death is to be over-come, and we are to be raised 'incorruptible' and immortal in the resurrection. What we consider as the natural law of the universe will no longer be the way things operate. Of this future ontological transformation of the cosmos, the Risen Christ is the 'first-fruits' or prototype. This present fallen world, groaning in bondage to decay (*phthora*), will experience the 'freedom of the glory of the children of God' (Rom. 8:21). Of course, when we think of 'the new heavens and the new earth', we are not thinking of a totally new creation *ex nihilo*; we are thinking of the new creation coming out of the old as the new resurrection body of Christ came out of his tomb. We are to think therefore of both continuity and dis-continuity. The changes, while cosmic in the sense that the same physical laws obtain throughout the universe in its vastness, may be subtle and would presumably particularly affect human life and being on this planet.

Of course, these are all statements of faith made from the vantage point of revelation. They are not conclusions drawn from the investigations of the natural sciences. Nevertheless the insight of post-Einstein science that space and time are dimensions of the universe, not an ontologically prior absolute framework within which the universe exists, helps us to see that space-time itself will be affected by the renewal of the cosmos, the new creation, the new heavens and the new earth. The thought is staggering of course, especially for those whose God is (as J. B. Phillips put it) 'too small', but only within such a breathtaking view of *cosmic*

Footnote 28 (*cont.*)

Pascal, to Barth and Einstein). Cf. *Space, Time and Incarnation* (Oxford: OUP, 1969), pp. 52–90.

redemption does the Christian hope of the resurrection of the body make any sense. Or to put that the other way, the physical resurrection of Jesus has cosmic implications.

It is in the light of this New Testament eschatology (the doctrine of the Last Things), that we must re-conceive 'protology' (the doctrine of the First Things). If we are to speak of the 'age to come' (which we may call 'redeemed time') and 'this present evil age' ('fallen time'), we should also speak of the age before the Fall ('unfallen time'). For as an ontological change will come to the creation with the *parousia*, rescuing it from futility and bondage to decay (*phthora*), so we conceive that an ontological change, subtle perhaps but profound, occurred for humanity and the world at the Fall, subjecting humanity to death and decay (*phthora*).

But as the *parousia* is known only through revelation and is unknown to natural human insight, so that human science and knowledge assume the continued existence of the universe in the present conditions which we observe, so the Fall can only be known through revelation. It is not accessible to human science and to critical history. It is not and *cannot* be known by natural human insight, research and investigation. By definition, 'secular' knowledge is limited to this *saeculum*, this *aeon*, this 'present evil Age'. Empirical, historical investigation is *incapable* of taking account of either the *parousia* or the Fall. Neither can they be comprehended *within* its timeline for they mark the ending and the beginning of this age and thus transcend it. By definition, they cannot be contained *within* it. Although the Fall was a real event, and the *parousia* will be a real event, neither is accessible to empirical natural scientific investigation. In short, from the viewpoint of natural science and the historical-critical method, both of which methodologically project present conditions into the past and the future, the world must look as if it always has been fallen and always will be.

Possibly this is what we are to understand from the angel with the flaming sword: there is no way back into Eden. Creation and Fall are inaccessible to scientific or historical investigation. Yet we have to affirm from Holy Scripture that the Fall was a temporal event and that there is a timeline from Adam to Christ within the fallen age.

If all this is counter-intuitive and mind-blowing, it is no more so than the great new hypotheses of modern science such as Einstein's theory of relativity. That light should bend or that the universe began in a miniscule primeval singularity and is expanding, that atoms could be split or nuclear bombs be built, even that heavy metal objects should fly or men land on the moon, even (going back to Copernicus) that the earth revolves around the sun – all of these would have been dismissed as absurd according to the intuition and commonsense of earlier generations. Therefore, while it may be counter-intuitive to suggest that the Fall was a real event which profoundly affected the time-space world, but is inaccessible to scientific or historical research, and while such a conception is drawn from revelation (*kata pneuma*) and not scientific observation (*kata sarka*), it is a theological hypothesis worth considering.

Death

We must address however the specific issue of death, for it is part of the historic Christian doctrine of the Fall, based on Genesis 3 and Romans 5 particularly, that 'death came through sin' (Rom. 5:12). This seems to fly in the face of scientific investigation of the primeval world, but we need to begin with the logic of this assertion *within biblical and Christian theology.*

The logic is that death is the consequence of alienation from the Source and Origin of life. Cut off from the Creator, humanity cannot but disintegrate. Here we come again to the key concept of corruption, meaning disintegration or decay (*phthora*) of the human *physis* which we have seen in Paul's thought (Rom. 8:21; 1 Cor. 15:42), and which was picked up by the Greek Fathers. Humanity, the crown of creation, is now the subject of decay, disease and disintegration leading to death. Disease and senility result from disintegration, the decay of the psychosomatic unity. As such, it is both a consequence and a judgment. Death passed to all 'because all sinned' (Rom. 5:12). Both the personal and the corporate dimension are here. Humanity (*bāśār, sarx*) is thus fallen in that it is mortal, perishing, disintegrating. Death is at work in our members. And because humanity, the crown of creation, is dying, all creation is affected, the beasts of the field and the principalities and powers in the heavens. All creation is subject to bondage, crying out for the glorious liberty of the sons of God.

This is the emphasis of the Greek Fathers, especially the Alexandrians, that the Fall is not *only* a spiritual-ethical matter, it is also an *ontological* matter. Humanity's very *being* is affected. The effect is not simply external, nor is it confined to the 'soul' or 'spirit'; it means disintegration and death for our whole *physis*. Humanity is doomed to die. We are *weakened* in every aspect of our being: spiritual, physical, intellectual and ethical. We are subject to *deprivatio*, deprived of life because we are deprived of communion with God. The fallenness is so radical that it affects our whole being. We cannot be patched up or cured. Fallen, mortal humanity must die in order to be raised again to immortality as an *integer*, an integrated whole.

That last comment makes it clear that this doctrine of death as a result of the Fall is in fact a corollary of the Christian doctrine of resurrection, which of course is centred on the resurrection of Christ. This is in fact the context within which death and decay are understood in 1 Corinthians 15. There Paul views mortal, fallen humanity from the viewpoint of the resurrection. And as the first letter of John adds, it is the resurrection of Jesus which reveals what we shall be like: 'We will be like him, for we shall see him as he is' (1 John 3:2).

It was from that viewpoint that Athanasius and the other Greek Fathers insisted that the Son of God took our *mortal* humanity, mortal as a result of the Fall. Athanasius does not mean, of course (as we have already made clear), that the Son of God took fallen humanity in the sense that he was subject to the *depravatio*, the *vitium* or defilement of sin. For one thing, this particular doctrine of human sinfulness was only fully developed later by Augustine. But Athanasius and the Greek Fathers were clear that in the very act of taking our fallen humanity from his mother, a member of Adam's fallen race, he sanctified it so that he was sinless.[29] This

---

29. Athanasius, *Contra Arianos*, Discourse I, 43 (*NPNF*, 2nd series, vol. 4, p. 331); Discourse II, 55, 56, 61, 66, 73, 76 (ibid., pp. 378, 38, 384, 390); III, 32,33 (ibid., p. 411f.). Gregory of Nyssa, *Antirrheticus adversus Apollinarem*, 26; Migne, *Patrologia Graeca*, vol. 45, 26. This is not available in English but a translation of a key passage will be found in J. H. Srawley, 'St Gregory of Nyssa on the Sinlessness of Christ', *Journal of Theological Studies* 7 (1906),

sanctification or regeneration of our human 'flesh' (i.e. humanity, human nature) was carried through continuously throughout his obedient, sacrificial and therefore sinless life, and was brought to its climax and conclusion in his sacrificial death. But it was still 'flesh', mortal humanity, weakened by the fall, *our* disintegrating, decaying, mortal humanity. The Greek Fathers argued that he had to take *that* humanity, *our* humanity in order to raise it incorruptible, undecaying, immortal and imperishable in his resurrection. Our bodies shall be like his glorious body in the resurrection precisely because it was *our* weakened, decaying humanity ('flesh') which he took to raise it immortal *in himself,* when he rose as the prototype of the new humanity.

It is as a corollary of this Christian understanding of resurrection that we have to affirm that death was a consequence of the Fall. At its heart it was a spiritual/ethical event, but it had *ontological* consequences, consequences for our very being and existence. We have no independent source of being or existence, no inherent immortality of the soul or anything else (as Platonism and Platonized Christianity claim) which we hold in independence from God. Cut off from the Source and Origin of life and being, our very existence was called into question.

Given that the doctrine of the resurrection is as central to Christian faith as the doctrine of the cross, Christian theology is bound to claim that death was a consequence of the Fall. However, we are still left with some options as to how we construe that. To repeat an earlier point which is particularly relevant here, we must avoid the folly of thinking of the doctrines of the Christian faith, such as the doctrine of creation, as if they were scientific theories, as in the absurdity of so-called 'creation science'. That is a muddled way of thinking which confuses two different levels of understanding and discourse, that which is by revelation (*kata pneuma*) and that which is by natural human insight (*kata sarka*). We must try

---

Footnote 29 (*cont.*)

> pp. 434–441. It is at this point that Edward Irving departed from the Fathers by thinking of 'the flesh' as sinful in itself and so writing of the 'sinful' humanity of Christ.

to relate the two levels, but we must not confuse them. Rather we must allow natural science and theological science each to work out its own logic in its own integrity without interference from the other. But having done so, it may be possible to draw *tentative* lines of connection, or to choose between equally possible options in a way which 'fits' the other discipline. One option which conflicts most flagrantly with modern science is to say that all death, human and animal, was the result of the Fall. A second option which may therefore be preferable is to say that, while the two narratives of human origins, that of Holy Scripture and that of natural science, must not be conflated, it is possible to interpret Christian doctrine as speaking only of *human* death as a result of the Fall. A third option is to go further and speak only of human death *as we know it*. One may speculate (as Calvin does) that the intention of God before the Fall was a benign translation from this scene of time to his nearer presence without the decay and death with which we are familiar.[30]

But at this point, we have gone beyond firm doctrine into an area where at present we can only hypothesize. We must hold to the key methodological point that over-hasty connections between the scientific story of humanity and the biblical story, not to say outright conflation of the two, must be resisted. We must be prepared to accept that there are things we do not yet know and that in the meantime we have to hold the two stories in tension. Indeed, that is the implication for our understanding of human beginnings which arises out of the paradoxical New Testament eschatology of the *already* and the *not yet*.

Sin

Our sketch of a doctrine of the Fall brings us back then to consider briefly the implications of all this for hamartiology, the doctrine of sin, and particularly, original sin. Having clarified the ten 'facets' in the concept of original sin, and having sketched a proposal for the doctrine of the Fall, are there any implications to draw in a positive theological articulation of this doctrine? One positive point to make

---

30. See his commentary on Genesis 2:17.

is that we must affirm the distinction between *acts of sin* and a *condition* of sinfulness: sin as *act* and sin as *condition*. It is the latter which is frequently referred to by the Augustinian term, 'original sin'.

Acts of sin

Here two traditional theological definitions of an act of sin which have been debated by Evangelicals have to be taken into account. There is the definition of Answer 14 of the Westminster Shorter Catechism, that classical Calvinist statement, that sin is 'any want of conformity unto or transgression of the law of God'. But the paradoxical reality of sin requires another definition, 'a voluntary transgression of a known law', the definition used (though not devised) by John Wesley. Wesley did not include involuntary transgressions (unwitting mistakes, failings, errors and offences due to lack of wisdom or knowledge) as 'sins properly so called', and yet he held that they need atonement. That clearly implies that they are part of the problem, part of the barrier between us and God. For the Westminster men, involuntary transgressions *are* sins.

It is surely best to view these not as rival definitions, but as complementary. We need them *both* in order to articulate our understanding of this paradoxical reality. Wesley's definition draws on the long tradition going back to Augustine and rooted in the Old and New Testaments that sin is rebellion. It is deliberate, intentional, voluntary, wilful disobedience, and so is culpable. In the realm of pastoral theology (and that was what concerned Wesley as a pastoral theologian and spiritual mentor), this definition was necessary in order to make it clear that Christians do not live daily in deliberate, outward, flagrant sin, intentionally and flagrantly flouting the law of God day in and day out. That was the way in which Wesley understood that otherwise terrifying text, 'Those who have been born of God do not sin' (1 John 3:9). Christians do not daily lie, steal, cheat or otherwise live in voluntary, intentional, flagrant disobedience to the Ten Commandments. The Reformed pastor will lead his people in confession of sin each week, but if he is caught in the act of embezzlement or adultery, he will not be in his pulpit confessing his sins the following Sunday! All traditions therefore in fact recognize the validity of Wesley's definition as part of the doctrine of sin. To say that we sin in word, thought and deed every day (the Westminster view) can therefore be misleading and spiritually damaging in that, if unqualified, it may lead a Christian into antinomianism, deliberately disobeying God daily, yet claiming still to be his child. It may lead to carelessness or a false belief in one's own regeneration even though it is clearly contradicted by one's life.

But on the other hand, the wider definition ('any want of conformity to the law of God') makes it clear that we must daily pray as the Lord directed us: 'Forgive us our trespasses.' As Wesley said, we daily need the atonement of the blood of Christ, for, although he will not use the term 'sin' (since to his Aristotelian logic, that would contradict 1 John 3:9), he *does* use 'transgressions' as a wider category. The regenerate Christian does not live in 'sin', that is in deliberate, wilful flouting of the known law of God in ways which are immoral ('voluntary transgressions'), and yet she or he needs daily repentance and confession of falling short and of 'involuntary transgressions'. Repentance in that sense must be a life-long attitude. It is not that we deliberately and flagrantly commit sin (murder, steal, lie, cheat) and repent day in and day out, but that we recognize daily that even our best endeavours fall short of what we could be, and that many of our motives may be confused and indeed murky. We daily transgress the perfect law of God by our errors and compromises and failures in thought and practice. Although not voluntarily transgressing in ways which are deliberately immoral, we fail as Christians by doing what we ought not to do, or not doing the good we ought to do. According to this wider definition of sin, there is no such thing as *sinless* perfection in this life. In daily confession therefore we rely as Christians not on our own righteousness, but Christ living and reigning within.

Both definitions of acts of sin are therefore necessary to do justice to the paradoxical reality which sin is. It is wilful blindness. We will not obey because we cannot, but we cannot because we will not. We are enslaved in our freedom; we are simultaneously responsible but helpless.

Original sin
Such a paradoxical understanding of acts of sin coheres with the paradoxical understanding of original sin. Here the Augustinian

definition must be tested against Scripture and not read into Scripture. The emphasis on the universal sin of humanity has to be seen as a corollary of the doctrine of grace. It is because we hold that salvation is only by grace through the sacrifice of Christ, that we have to have a doctrine of sin which includes not only individual acts which need pardon through that sacrifice (the aspect clearly emphasized in the Western Anselmic tradition), but one which has a more comprehensive and holistic understanding of what sin is. The atonement must be understood to bring salvation not only in the form of forgiveness for our acts of sin, but also in the form of ultimate deliverance from original sin in *all* its aspects. Our doctrine of sin therefore must include not only individual transgressions but also the corporate reality of a spiritually diseased and corrupt human race comprising individuals, organic groups (families, tribes, nations) and voluntary groups (business partnerships, companies, political parties, trade unions, social classes) who are determined by individual or group self-interest. Here are both the corporate and the motivational dimensions of sin which in many instances can become truly demonic in the form of militarism and racism, the victimization of the weak, the abuse of children and the marginalized. Despite the bizarre theories of Augustine on heredity and lust (which may be laid aside as not integral to the doctrine), the doctrine of original sin which he formulated on the basis of Holy Scripture and as a necessary component of the gospel of grace is surely the most realistic portrayal of the reality of human sin. Here we see not only individual acts, but the deep inner reality of sin in the human heart, and also the reality of sin as social, political and economic.

'*Original sin*' *as the* reatus *or guilt of sin*. Augustine taught that we all shared corporately in Adam's guilt. Here we do not need any theory of genetic transmission to affirm the biblical view of the corporate solidarity of humanity. To say that we share in Adam's guilt is to affirm *corporate responsibility*, and this follows if we see that there is not only the personal or individual aspect of humanity, but there is a corporate dimension. Augustine taught that this inherited guilt was washed away in baptism but that is surely a misleadingly individualistic way of putting it. The point is better put thus: that the corporate guilt of humanity (guilt 'in Adam') was dealt with on the cross by the Second Adam. The cross cancelled humanity's corporate guilt before God. In the new head of the race, humanity as such is reconciled to God. Therefore, as Wesley put it, no one will be condemned for Adam's sin.[31] It is this prior fact to which baptism witnesses.

'*Original sin*' *as the* vitium, *the vice or disease of sin*. Augustine saw this as the defilement passed down through the generations by the lust involved in the conception of each human being. While this theory as to the mechanism is quite unbiblical, the idea of the *vitium* as *concupiscentia* should not be rejected, once it is interpreted not as sexual lust merely, but as *all* self-centred desire. 'Concupiscence' must be understood as the New Testament concept of *epithymia*, and a valid interpretation of the *phronēma tēs sarkos*, the 'mind that is set on the flesh', that is, what we might call the 'self-centred mind-set'. However, this idea must be clearly differentiated from the physical desires or 'drives' listed by psychologists and usually including hunger, sex, aggression, among others. It is not the basic physiologically-based desires which are sinful: they are inherent in humanity as created. It is the *self-centred direction* of these natural desires which is *concupiscentia*, the conscious turning inward of the motives on oneself so that the rational life of love in community is undermined by natural desires which are no longer under the disciplined control of love for God and neighbour.

This distinction is a most important one which arises from an understanding of Christ as fully human, sharing the infirmity of our flesh so that 'in every respect [he] has been tested as we are, yet without sin' (Heb. 4:15). Living human life in the body as we

---

31. *The Letters of John Wesley*, ed. John Telford, vol. VI (London: Epworth Press, 1931), pp. 239f.: 'That, "by the offence of one, judgment came upon all men" (all born into the world) "unto condemnation," is an undoubted truth, and affects every infant as well as every adult person. But it is equally true that, "by the righteousness of one, the free gift came upon all men" (all born into the world, infant or adult) "unto justification." Therefore no infant ever was or ever will be "sent to hell for the guilt of Adam's sin," seeing it is cancelled by the righteousness of Christ as soon as they are sent into the world.'

do, he had the same physiological drives; to deny that is to deny his humanity and fall into the heresy of docetism. Sharing our flesh and bodily existence, he was subject to temptations as fierce as ours, indeed (it has been argued) fiercer, for he resisted temptation consistently. But whereas for us, life in the flesh and the pressures of the physiologically-based desires lead to the *vitium* of self-centred living, in him it did not. Subject to the same pressures to be self-centred, to live to gratify himself and glorify himself and justify himself and satisfy himself, he alone, living in the power of the Holy Spirit, did not succumb. The self-centred mind-set, the *phronēma tēs sarkos*, was never ever formed in him as it is in us.

All this helps us to see what the *vitium* of *concupiscentia* is in us. In us, the natural desires are twisted into self-centred desire (*epithymia*), the desire to have, to possess, to control, to enjoy for ourselves, living for self-enjoyment, self-glory, self-fulfilment, trusting in our own self-sufficiency, living in self-sovereignty. This is the *phronēma tēs sarkos*, the self-centred mind-set, the carnal mind which is 'hostile to God' (Rom. 8:7). It is not a 'thing' or entity, but a condition of mind and heart.

Once we lay aside therefore the peculiar hypothesis of Augustine about the role of human sexuality in the transmission of original sin, his doctrine is seen to be a profound and perceptive theological development of the doctrine of sin from Holy Scripture. It links together the primeval event of the Fall and the contemporary reality of sin in human society, sin as act and sin as condition, sin in individual motivation and sin as paradoxical reality in the social, political and economic structures of corporate human life. Not surprisingly, since human sexuality is so basic to our motivation, sin is indeed to be seen at its most destructive precisely there, but it is also to be seen in our warped desires to possess and to dominate.

Conclusion

The doctrines of the Fall and original sin are therefore a necessary and indispensable part of Christian theology. They are clear implications of the doctrine of salvation by grace and without them historic Christianity becomes incoherent and is quickly turned into another gospel, one which is more or less Humanist. Since Darwin, that has created an apologetic problem for the Church, but Christian theology must resist the temptation to be driven by apologetics. If there are tensions with the story told by modern science, we must not fall into the trap of conflating the two stories, but live with the tension while working at ways of resolving it. It may be that, given the paradox of the two ages, 'this present evil age' and 'the age to come', we may not be able to see the resolution of the tension until the kingdom comes in glory and power. But to counterbalance the apologetic problem of living with the tension, there is the point that the Christian doctrine of original sin is the most realistic of all doctrines. Humanity is paradoxically both the crown of creation and, sadly, a living contradiction. No other perspective on option offers such a profoundly realistic picture of both the glory and the depravity, the altruistic idealism and the demonic hatred, the sublime beauty and the bestiality and cruelty of human existence today. That is surely an apologetic advantage.

6. IRENAEUS ON THE FALL AND ORIGINAL SIN

A. N. S. Lane

Western theology was for some 1,400 years dominated by Augustine's perspective on the Fall and original sin. Since the time of the Enlightenment this dominance has been broken, but his influence remains considerable. Those who have wished to challenge Augustine have often found in Irenaeus an alternative and more acceptable model. Because Irenaeus, unlike Augustine, wrote very little about these matters it has proved easy for modern theologians to read their ideas into him and to use him as a sounding board for their own theories.[1] In this paper we will aim to do two things. First, we shall examine some disputed points in Irenaeus's theology and clarify what he actually taught. Secondly, we shall draw a contrast between the Irenaean and Augustinian models of the Fall.

---

1. The Dominican theologian Denis Minns is particularly guilty of this, in his *Irenaeus* (London: Geoffrey Chapman, 1994).

Irenaeus's teaching on the Fall

Recapitulation

Irenaeus is known especially for his doctrine of recapitulation, which is based upon the parallels between Adam and Christ, the two heads (not his term) of the human race. We fell in solidarity with Adam and we rise through solidarity with Christ. Irenaeus, like the Bible in general and Paul in particular, devotes far more attention to our salvation in Christ than to our Fall in Adam. But the importance of the parallel for Irenaeus means that our Fall in Adam is not some minor side issue that can be removed from his theology without major implications for the rest.

Adam and Eve not created perfect

Irenaeus held that Adam and Eve were not created perfect and explains why this should be so. He argues that it is not possible for the newly-created to be perfect because Adam was infantile and inexperienced in perfect discipline. 'It was possible for God to have made man perfect from the first, but man could not receive this [perfection] being as yet an infant' (*Against Heresies* [*AH*] 4:38:1).[2] 'God had power at the beginning to grant perfection to man; but as the latter was only recently created, he could not possibly have received it, [n]or even if he had received it, could he have contained it, [n]or containing it, could he have retained it' (*AH* 4:38:2). Irenaeus draws the parallel with the way that Christ also passed through the state of infancy, but then weakens his case by qualifying this with 'although He was perfect', while Hebrews much more boldly affirms that he needed to learn obedience and be made perfect (5:8–9). Furthermore, his argument is somewhat obscured in this passage as he switches between two different

---

2. Quotations from AH are from A. Roberts and J. Donaldson (eds.), *Ante-Nicene Fathers* [*ANF*], vol. 1 (Grand Rapids: Eerdmans, 1973 reprint). They have been checked for accuracy against the texts in *Sources Chrétiennes* [*SC*], vols. 100, 153, 211 (Paris: du Cerf, 1965, 1969, 1974). For a discussion of 4:38, see R. F. Brown, 'On the Necessary Imperfection of Creation: Irenaeus' *Adversus Haereses* IV, 38', *SJT* 28 (1975), pp. 17–25.

situations – Adam and Eve as originally created, without sin but not yet perfect because immature, and believers today who are in the process of sanctification and glorification, but not yet perfect because still tainted by sin:

> Now it was necessary that man should in the first instance be created; and having been created, should receive growth; and having received growth, should be strengthened; and having been strengthened, should abound; and having abounded, should recover [from the disease of sin]; and having recovered, should be glorified; and being glorified, should see his Lord (*AH* 4:38:3).[3]

His general argument appears to be that perfection needs to be the outcome of a process and this principle would therefore apply both to Adam and Eve as newly created and immature and to Christians as converted but not yet perfect:

> For it was necessary, at first, that nature should be exhibited; then, after that, that what was mortal should be conquered and swallowed up by immortality, and the corruptible by incorruptibility, and that man should be made after the image and likeness of God, having received the knowledge of good and evil (*AH* 4:38:4).

There are two misunderstandings that must be dispelled at this point. First, not to be perfect is not the same as to be sinful. The mainstream tradition has always seen Adam and Eve in the garden as on probation, undergoing a time of testing, but not as sinful before they fell for the serpent's temptation. Augustine summed this up with his famous contrast: Adam and Eve, as created, were able to sin and also able not to sin (*posse peccare et posse non peccare*). In the age to come we will be perfect and no longer able to sin

---

3. The French translation sees a reference to becoming adult and reproducing (*SC* 100, p. 957): 'should be strengthened' becomes 'devînt adulte' and 'should abound' becomes 'se multipliât'. Both translations are linguistically possible, but the French does not fit well into the overall argument of the sentence.

(*non posse peccare*).[4] Minns is at best misleading to state that (for Irenaeus) 'Adam did not fall from a state of original justice'. He goes on to state that '[Adam] was created a "little one", by a God who always intended that he should grow into the full stature of Christ'.[5] This is true in that Adam and Eve as created were not yet perfect or even mature, but not if it implies that they were created unrighteous or sinful. Their initial state was one of innocence.

Related to this, secondly, is the belief, also consistently held by the mainstream tradition, that the end is vastly more than simply the restoration of things to their original state. One only has to compare Genesis 2 with Revelation 21 – 22 to see this. Unfortunately there are those recently who have imagined that the traditional position is that salvation is simply restoration. Moltmann claims that, only to reject this supposed tradition.[6] He was right to reject it; wrong to suppose that it was the traditional view. With reference to Irenaeus, Robert Brown has made the same mistake. He argues that Irenaeus's assumption of Adam's imperfection 'cannot readily be assimilated into the usual Christian theological formulation, according to which salvation is the restoration of a person to the status of the original created human nature, as it was before exposure to evil'.[7] Apart from Origen I can think of no serious Christian writer who has ever imagined such a thing.

Irenaeus is not identical to Augustine on this point, but where they do *not* differ is in drawing a contrast between the time of trial and probation in the garden and the perfection that will come at the end.

Original likeness?

Irenaeus taught, as has almost the entire Christian tradition, that Adam and Eve were originally created in God's image and after his likeness (Gen 1:26).[8] Or did he? There are a few passages which

---

4. Augustine, *Rebuke and Grace*, 12:33.

5. Minns, *Irenaeus*, p. 136.

6. Cf. J. Moltmann, *The Coming of God* (London: SCM, 1996), pp. 261–267.

7. Brown, 'Necessary Imperfection of Creation', p. 19.

8. *AH* 3:18:1; 3:23:1; 5:2:1; 5:10:1; 5:16:2. Cf. G. Wingren, *Man and the*

have been read to imply that Adam was created in God's image but that the likeness was something which he had yet to attain.[9] Let us review these passages.

> And then, again, this Word was manifested when the Word of God was made man, assimilating Himself to man, and man to Himself, so that by means of his resemblance to the Son, man might become precious to the Father. For in times long past, it was *said* that man was created after the image of God, but it was not [actually] *shown*; for the Word was as yet invisible, after whose image man was created, Wherefore also he did easily lose the similitude. When, however, the Word of God became flesh, He confirmed both these: for He both showed forth the image truly, since He became Himself what was His image; and He re-established the similitude after a sure manner, by assimilating man to the invisible Father through means of the visible Word (*AH* 5:16:2).

This passage states that the image was not yet visible at the beginning, but this does not mean that Adam was not in God's likeness. The point is, rather, that the divine Word, God's image, had not yet become incarnate. The reference to man *losing* the similitude and to Christ re-establishing it clearly implies that Adam was created after the likeness of God, not just in his image.

There are three other passages that refer to the likeness to God as something to which we are striving, through the work of the Spirit. These do indeed present the likeness as an eschatological goal, but the context is our loss of the original likeness through sin, not that Adam and Eve lacked the likeness when created. That is clear from the fact that the first of these passages begins by affirming that man was made in the likeness of God and then goes on to argue that without the Spirit we lack this likeness.

Footnote 8 (*cont.*)

  Incarnation: A Study in the Biblical Theology of Irenaeus (Edinburgh and London: Oliver and Boyd, 1959), pp. 14–26.

 9. E.g. by John Hick, *Evil and the God of Love* (London: Collins, 1968), pp. 217–218, 289–290, 323.

For by the hands of the Father, that is, by the Son and the Holy Spirit, man, and not [merely] a part of man, was made in the likeness of God. . . . But when the spirit here blended with the soul is united to [God's] handiwork, the man is rendered spiritual and perfect because of the outpouring of the Spirit, and this is he who was made in the image and likeness of God. But if the Spirit be wanting to the soul, he who is such is indeed of an animal nature, and being left carnal, shall be an imperfect being, possessing indeed the image [of God] in his formation (*in plasmate*), but not receiving the similitude through the Spirit; and thus is this being imperfect (*AH* 5:6:1).

The next passage makes no explicit reference to sin, but the context is the process of salvation, and to deduce from the reference to likeness as our eschatological goal that Adam and Eve were not created after God's likeness, is arbitrarily to put Irenaeus in conflict both with Genesis 1:26 and with his own explicit teaching in many other places.

But we do now receive a certain portion of His Spirit, tending towards perfection, and preparing us for incorruption, being little by little accustomed to receive and bear God. . . . For if the earnest, gathering man into itself, does even now cause him to cry, 'Abba, Father,' what shall the complete grace of the Spirit effect, which shall be given to men by God? It will render us like unto Him, and accomplish the will of the Father; for it shall make man after the image and likeness of God (*AH* 5:8:1).

The same consideration applies to the final passage:

For there is the one Son, who accomplished His Father's will; and one human race also in which the mysteries of God are wrought, 'which the angels desire to look into;' and they are not able to search out the wisdom of God, by means of which His handiwork, confirmed and incorporated with His Son, is brought to perfection; that His offspring, the First-begotten Word, should descend to the creature (*facturam*), that is, to what had been moulded (*plasma*), and that it should be contained by Him; and, on the other hand, the creature should contain the Word, and ascend to Him, passing beyond the angels, and be made after the image and likeness of God (*AH* 5:36:3).

There are two opposite errors to be avoided in expounding Irenaeus at this point. On the one hand, it is wrong to suggest that Christ does no more than restore what Adam lost. The contrast between initial innocence and final perfection refutes this. But on the other hand it is equally wrong to suggest that Christ simply supplies what Adam lacked at creation, thus eliminating the Fall. Adam was not created perfect, but he did have a likeness to God that he lost and which Christ restores, albeit to a much fuller extent than the original.[10]

Childhood

Irenaeus famously states that Adam and Eve in the garden were but children. In *Proof of the Apostolic Preaching*, Irenaeus states that in Eden Adam 'was a little one; for he was a child and had need to grow so as to come to his full perfection'. He was as yet 'a little one, and his discretion still undeveloped, wherefore also he was easily misled by the deceiver' (12). In *Against Heresies* he argues similarly. Adam and Eve as newly created were 'infantile', man was 'as yet an infant' (*AH* 4:38:1–2).

What does Irenaeus mean by this? First, it should be noted that Theophilus of Antioch had already taught the same: 'Adam, being yet an infant in age, was on this account as yet unable to receive knowledge worthily . . . [God] wished man, infant as he was, to remain for some time longer simple and sincere.'[11] So what do Theophilus and Irenaeus have in mind? Kelly states that (for Irenaeus) in Paradise Adam 'was morally, spiritually and intellectually a child'.[12] That much is uncontroversial, but did Irenaeus also understand Adam to be *physically* a child? The situation is unusual in that this is not a question of age. Clearly Adam and Eve had only been in existence for a short time but equally clearly they were not still in nappies. Traditionally they have been portrayed as youthful but sexually mature. This Irenaeus appears to deny:

---

10. Wingren, *Man and Incarnation*, pp. 20, 26–28, gives the analogy of a child, who cannot yet talk, losing the capacity of speech through an injury.

11. Theophilus, *To Autolycus* 2:25 (*ANF*, vol. 2), p. 104.

12. J. N. D. Kelly, *Early Christian Doctrines* (London: Adam & Charles Black, 1968), p. 171.

And even as [Eve], having indeed a husband, Adam, but being
nevertheless as yet a virgin (for in Paradise 'they were both naked,
and were not ashamed,' inasmuch as they, having been created a
short time previously, had no understanding of the procreation of
children: for it was necessary that they should first come to adult
age [*adolescere*], and then multiply from that time onward) . . . (*AH*
3:22:4).

This does suggest that Irenaeus saw them as not yet having
reached puberty. The Greek and Latin words do not need to refer
to that,[13] and it could be that the reference is to the innocence of
those as yet unaware of the facts of life, but it is most likely that
he did think of them as sexually immature. In *Proof of the Apostolic
Preaching* he also states that they kissed each other and embraced
with the innocence of childhood (14).

Fall inevitable?

Perhaps the most controversial claim that Minns makes for
Irenaeus is that sin was inevitable:

> Irenaeus does not allow the possibility that all human beings might, from
> the beginning, freely and always have chosen the good instead of evil.
> As he sees it, the only possibilities are a world in which human beings
> are free to choose between good and evil and, because of their moral
> immaturity, *do sometimes choose evil*, and a world in which human beings
> have no power of choice between good and evil but are determined by a
> natural necessity to do good.[14]

---

13. And in *ANF* are translated differently in 4:38:3 (see n. 2, above), but just
    as the context there pointed against the reference to puberty, so here
    it points towards it. Mary Ann Donovan, *One Right Reading? A Guide to
    Irenaeus* (Collegeville: Liturgical Press, 1997) states that Irenaeus's 'point is
    not physical but moral childhood' (p. 132). Wingren, *Man and Incarnation*,
    pp. 26–38, has a lengthy discussion of Adam's 'childhood', but without
    addressing this particular issue.

14. Minns, *Irenaeus*, p. 75, my emphasis.

This is indeed a bold claim. The Christian tradition has all but universally affirmed what Minns portrays Irenaeus as denying. Augustine most explicitly teaches that Adam had the possibility not to sin[15] and held that the Fall was foreknown and permitted by God but not positively ordained.[16] Calvin famously went further and claimed that Adam fell because God decreed it, his *decretum horribile*,[17] but even he held that Adam fell solely by his own will, of his free choice, having the power not to sin.[18] So to affirm that sin was inevitable would be to fly in the face of the tradition, though Irenaeus himself obviously predated that tradition. Given the seriousness of the charge it is surprising that this claim is not backed up by appeal to any specific passage but comes rather as an extrapolation from the general account of Irenaeus's teaching on this matter.

Is there anything in Irenaeus to support such a claim? First, he teaches that Adam sinned because of his 'infancy'. In *Proof of the Apostolic Preaching*, he states that 'the man was a little one, and his discretion still undeveloped, wherefore also he was easily misled by the deceiver' (12). Related to this is Irenaeus's teaching in *Against Heresies* that man was not created perfect (*AH* 4:38), though the specific implication of being prone to being misled is not drawn out. More serious is the argument that it is necessary to have the knowledge of both good and evil in order to make an informed choice of the good. This is an ambiguous section that can be read more than one way. On the one hand, Irenaeus appears to teach that it is necessary to have a first-hand knowledge of evil in order to choose the good:

> Wherefore [man] has also had a twofold experience [of good and evil], possessing knowledge of both kinds, that with discipline he may make choice of the better things. But how, if he had no knowledge of the contrary, could he have had instruction in that which is good? For there is thus a surer and an undoubted comprehension of matters submitted to us

---

15. Augustine, *Rebuke and Grace*, 12:33.
16. Augustine, *City of God*, 12:22.
17. John Calvin, *Institutes of the Christian Religion*, 3:23:7.
18. Calvin, *Institutes*, 1:15:8.

than the mere surmise arising from an opinion regarding them. For just as the tongue receives experience of sweet and bitter by means of tasting, and the eye discriminates between black and white by means of vision, and the ear recognises the distinctions of sounds by hearing; so also does the mind, receiving through the experience of both the knowledge of what is good, become more tenacious of its preservation, by acting in obedience to God: in the first place, casting away, by means of repentance, disobedience, as being something disagreeable and nauseous; and afterwards coming to understand what it really is, that it is contrary to goodness and sweetness, so that the mind may never even attempt to taste disobedience to God. But if any one do shun the knowledge of both these kinds of things, and the twofold perception of knowledge, he unawares divests himself of the character of a human being (*AH* 4:39:1).

It is not hard to see how such an interpretation would seriously undermine Irenaeus's theology. If someone without first-hand experience of evil is unable to make a genuine choice of the good and has divested themselves of the character of a human being, where does that leave Christ? The whole idea of recapitulation is precisely that Christ became human like us and chose good where Adam chose evil. So is there an alternative interpretation? Just before the passage quoted, Irenaeus states:

Man has received the knowledge of good and evil. It is good to obey God, and to believe in Him, and to keep His commandment, and this is the life of man; as not to obey God is evil, and this is his death. Since God, therefore, gave [to man] such mental power (*magnanimitatem*) man knew both the good of obedience and the evil of disobedience, that the eye of the mind, receiving experience of both, may with judgment make choice of the better things; and that he may never become indolent or neglectful of God's command; and learning by experience that it is an evil thing which deprives him of life, that is, disobedience to God, may never attempt it at all, but that, knowing that what preserves his life, namely, obedience to God, is good, he may diligently keep it with all earnestness (*AH* 4:39:1).

This might indicate that by the knowledge of good and evil Irenaeus meant an intellectual awareness, not first-hand knowledge.

This is a more likely interpretation in that the serpent promised Eve that they would be *like God*, knowing good and evil (Gen 3:5). Presumably God's knowledge of good and evil does not extend to doing evil. Also, Irenaeus speaks of the knowledge of good and evil in the context of final salvation in a way that would be inconceivable had he thought that it included the practice of evil:

> It was necessary, at first, that nature should be exhibited; then, after that, that what was mortal should be conquered and swallowed up by immortality, and the incorruptible by incorruptibility, and that man should be made after the image and likeness of God, having received the knowledge of good and evil (*AH* 4:38:4).

Genesis 1 – 3 symbolic?

Minns claims that Genesis 1 – 3 is, for Irenaeus, in part *symbolic* and that he is in this sense more in tune with modern understandings than is Augustine. He concedes that Irenaeus saw Adam and Eve as real individuals, but claims that he also assigned them a symbolic significance. 'Adam is able to symbolize the whole of humanity in its relationship with God. . . . Adam is never just an individual for Irenaeus; he symbolizes all humanity, because all humanity is descended from him.'[19] Clearly it is true that for Irenaeus Adam is much more than a mere individual, but to describe this 'much more' as symbolism is gravely misleading – and even more so when this is described as a 'modern' reading, implicitly suggesting that Irenaeus supports those who see Adam and Eve as purely symbolic. Adam, as well as being an individual in his own right, does have an added significance but this is real, not symbolic. Adam led the human race astray, introduced sin and disobedience and brought death upon the human race. Christ came to reverse all of these. Apart from the fact that Irenaeus does not talk of Adam in symbolic terms, the whole scheme of recapitulation, with the parallels between Adam and Christ, implies that Adam's significance for humanity is very real, not symbolic. Because of his emphasis on recapitulation, Irenaeus's theology is

---

19. Minns, *Irenaeus*, p. 58.

undermined more than most others by the suggestion of a non-historical Adam.

Original sin?

Clearly Irenaeus wrote vastly less about original sin than did Augustine. Thanks to the stimulus of Pelagius, Augustine was led to expound the topic in graphic detail, building on the much briefer statements by his predecessors. Lawson claims that 'Irenaeus did not therefore believe in Original Sin in the proper sense of the word'.[20] The truth or otherwise of this statement depends on what one understands by the 'proper sense' of original sin. The best approach will be to unpack what Irenaeus actually does say about three distinct issues – death, sinfulness and guilt.

No one doubts that Irenaeus saw Adam as inflicting death upon his descendants. That is so clearly taught in Scripture that even Pelagius did not deny it. One of the key points of recapitulation is that where Adam introduced death to the human race, Christ has brought life. But, following Paul, Irenaeus states not just that Adam made us mortal but also that he made us sinners. Through Adam's sin humanity is drawn into bondage to sin. 'By the disobedience of the one man . . . the many were made sinners, and forfeited life' (*AH* 3:18:7). Through his sin Adam fell into captivity to Satan and we his children are born into the same captivity (*AH* 3:23:2). Satan 'led us away captives in Adam' (*AH* 5:21:1).[21] Adam's descendants are not sinless people who have had a death penalty imposed upon them. But are they perhaps innocent people who have simply inherited a sinfulness imposed on them? Irenaeus states that just as we offended God in the first Adam, so we are reconciled in the second Adam. 'We were debtors to none other but to Him whose commandment we had transgressed at the beginning' (*AH* 5:16:3). It is we who 'sinned in the beginning', in Adam (*AH* 5:17:1).

---

20. J. Lawson, *The Biblical Theology of Saint Irenaeus* (London: Epworth, 1948), p. 216.

21. Wingren, *Man and Incarnation*, pp. 50–75, expounds the corruption and bondage of the human race, as taught by Irenaeus.

The stress in Irenaeus is upon Adam having introduced death into the human race, but it would be wrong to suppose that he saw the newborn as innocent or without sin. Such an approach would imply an individualism that is foreign to his very corporate concept of the first and second Adam. It is also belied by his few explicit statements on the topic. Although the ideas are massively under-developed compared with Augustine, the basic idea that we sinned in Adam and thus became sinners is there in Irenaeus.[22] To read into Irenaeus an individualistic concept of sin that excludes the corporate sin of the human race in Adam would be seriously to misread him. Again, Irenaeus is not explicit about original sin in the sense of a bias towards sin in the newborn, but he does affirm that through Adam's sin all people are born into bondage to Satan and it is not likely that this bondage excludes bondage to sin. Lawson goes too far when he states that for Irenaeus, 'sin is wrong moral choice and *not* inborn defect of nature'.[23] To present these as alternatives is to miss the nuance of the doctrine of original sin.

The nature of the Fall

What was the nature of the Fall? There is a contrast between the approaches of Augustine and Irenaeus,[24] which can be seen by asking three questions:

- Was the world perfect?
- Were Adam and Eve perfect?
- Were Adam and Eve immortal?

---

22. E. Osborn, *Irenaeus of Lyons* (Cambridge: CUP, 2001), p. 218, affirms Irenaeus's belief in original guilt.
23. Lawson, *Biblical Theology*, p. 222.
24. Hick, *Evil and the God of Love, passim*, famously contrasts what he calls the Augustinian and Irenaean type of theodicy, though it has been questioned how close the latter is to the actual teaching of Irenaeus. The contrast that I am drawing here is related to, but not identical to, Hick's.

Following Augustine, it became traditional to see Adam and Eve as inhabiting a perfect world. There was a tendency to think of them as immortal. At times they were seen as morally and intellectually all but perfect. The result was that Genesis 3 was understood as a fall from a great height. All of this creates intolerable tensions with the modern scientific view. The Garden of Eden becomes like the lost city of Atlantis, the scene of a primitive culture of great value. There are problems with the existence of death before the Fall. There are problems with the evolutionary account of human origins. If this were the sum of the problems then our loyalty to Scripture might lead us to question modern science. But there is a far more serious problem with the traditional view. It is not even scriptural! Let us review the above points individually.

Did Adam and Eve live in a perfect world? If so, how does this cohere with a view of 'nature red in tooth and claw' prior to *Homo sapiens*?[25] But it is not the Bible that tells us that animals were pacifists and vegetarians before the Fall. Isaiah 11:6-9 and other passages present a picture of harmony and peace in the animal kingdom, but this is a vision of the end, not the beginning. Apart from Origen, no Christian theologian of stature has fallen into the mistake of supposing that the end will simply be a restoration of the beginning. To give but one example, *posse non peccare* (the ability not to sin) is to be replaced by *non posse peccare* (the inability to sin). Furthermore, there are hints in Genesis 3 itself that the world was not perfect. Eve was tempted by the serpent. No further explanation is given, but the plain implication is that human sin was not the first rebellion against the Creator in the universe. This coheres with traditional teaching about the fall of Satan, though it would be wrong to read such a doctrine into Genesis 3.[26]

Again, Adam and Eve were expelled from the garden. Are we to understand by this that paradisal conditions were at that time confined to the garden? Genesis 2:8 and 3:23 could be taken to imply that. There are certainly no grounds for dogmatically stating that the whole world was at that stage perfect. It is important to

---

25. Tennyson, 'In Memoriam A.H.H.' (1849), line 56.
26. See H. Blocher, *In the Beginning* (Leicester: IVP, 1984), pp. 150–154.

distinguish between what is good and what is perfect. Jesus was always good, but he was made perfect (Heb. 5:9). Something that is part of the way through a process of development may be good (for that stage) but it is not yet perfect. Romans 8:18–25 might be cited in support of the claim that Adam's fall has ruined the whole universe. But what does this passage say? Does 'the creation' mean the whole universe or just the earth? Is the cause of the subjection *only* human sin or is it also angelic sin? Is the result of human sin understood as a sudden transformation of the nature of the creation or rather (to some extent at least) the effects of human sin in the ecological realm? This passage is patient of a variety of interpretations and it is rash without good grounds to impose on it a 'maximal' interpretation that unnecessarily conflicts with the scientific account.

Before the Fall Adam and Eve were not yet morally perfect. They were on probation. They had not yet sinned, but nor had they yet learned obedience. Their state was that of *posse non peccare* – they were able not to sin. They had not reached the state of *non posse peccare* – not being able to sin. Had they reached it, the Fall would have been impossible! It is therefore wrong to think of Adam and Eve as falling from a great moral height. Rather, they were setting out on a path of moral testing and at an early stage they took a wrong turn.

In fact the very language of 'fall' is itself misleading,[27] though at this late stage it is probably too late to do anything about it. Genesis 3 does not describe the 'fall' of humanity, which is more of a Gnostic idea. It would be more accurate to describe it as our 'coming of age'. The serpent promises that Adam and Eve will become 'like God, knowing good and evil' (v. 5). This was no idle boast since, according to the statement of God himself that is exactly what did happen (v. 22). What does this mean?[28] It cannot

---

27. Blocher, *In the Beginning*, pp. 135–136, also has misgivings.
28. See Blocher, *In the Beginning*, pp. 126–133 on the meaning of the phrase. See also C. Westermann, *Genesis 1–11. A Commentary* (London: SPCK, 1984), pp. 240–248; V. P. Hamilton, *The Book of Genesis Chapters 1–17* (Grand Rapids: Eerdmans, 1990), pp. 163–166.

mean omniscience, as some interpreters suggest, since that was manifestly not the outcome of the Fall. Nor can it mean the *experience* of doing both good and evil, since God does not have that. It must mean moral autonomy and independence, setting oneself up as one's own judge of what is right and wrong. This is precisely what Adam and Eve did. The serpent challenged them to become like God by setting themselves up as their own arbiters of good and evil, in opposition to God. This is the essence of sin – setting oneself up against God. Jesus was tempted to do this, but refused (Matt. 4:1–11; Phil. 2:5–11). Adam and Eve, by contrast, succumbed and launched out on a course of deliberate adult independence. This decision made them in that respect like God and it sums up very aptly the situation that the human race finds itself in today. For example, we have nuclear weapons, which confront us with an ethical situation in which we are some extent out of our depth. We have no choice but to grapple with the problem ourselves. Just as newly independent states now have to make their own decisions, so autonomous humanity is forced to grapple with this problem itself, to 'play God' with it.

Thus the first sin was a declaration of moral independence, a premature step into adult independence, a wrong turning which took us forward in the wrong direction rather than a fall from a state of perfection already achieved. At *this* point Irenaeus seems to be more perceptive than Augustine. The experience of Adam and Eve in Genesis 3 is reminiscent of the experience of puberty, of the 'loss of innocence' that comes with sexual awareness. This is only a comparison. There is no suggestion that the Fall involved sexual sin. But the point of the comparison is that the loss of innocence goes hand in hand with a step forward into a new realm of experience and a leaving behind of childhood. All of this is not to deny that the primal sin was a moral disaster with devastating implications. The point at issue is not the *seriousness* of the event. The question is whether Adam fell from a perfect state or, by overstepping the mark, set the human race on the wrong course and lost the way to perfection.

Were human beings immortal before the Fall? Genesis 3 and Romans 5 both blame death on the Fall. How can this be squared with an evolutionary account of the origins of life? It is important to note what Genesis does and does not say. Death is the penalty of sin, but it is not stated that Adam was immortal before he sinned. Clearly he was not since by definition an immortal being cannot die! Rather, he had access to the tree of life and this access was denied to him after his sin. The picture appears to be of an inherently mortal being that is offered the gift of eternal life. The Fall caused the human race to lose the *possibility* of eternal life. It will be clear that this picture does not clash with an evolutionary picture of human origins. Immortality is portrayed by Genesis as something that was held before us, to which we never attained. There is no need to postulate an immortal state of unfallen humanity. Genesis is at this point compatible with a picture of humanity emerging from a brutish origin. So, interestingly, is the anthropology of at least some of the early Fathers who, it need hardly be stated, cannot be accused of pandering to Darwin. Athanasius in his *De Incarnatione* sees two aspects of human creation, which he calls nature and grace. Nature is that which we have in common with irrational animals. To this God gave 'an added grace', his image, which involves rationality and freewill and which opens the way to immortality.[29] It can be seen how easily such a picture can be squared with the evolutionary account. Perhaps Protestants ought to be willing to look more sympathetically at the Catholic nature-supernature approach.[30] Calvin himself accepted the statement that the Fall results in humanity's loss of supernatural gifts and corruption of natural gifts.[31]

In the past some have held that unfallen humanity had attained to great intellectual and cultural achievements, encapsulated in the oft-quoted statement, 'An Aristotle was but the rubbish of an Adam, and Athens but the rudiments of paradise.'[32] A similar idea

---

29. Athanasius, *De Incarnatione*, ch. 3.

30. As suggested by A. Vos, *Aquinas, Calvin, and Contemporary Protestant Thought* (Grand Rapids: Eerdmans, 1985).

31. *Institutes* 2:2:12. In 2:2:4 he approves the aphorism, while rejecting the medieval misuse of it.

32. Attributed to R. South, and cited by Arthur Peake, *Christianity: Its Nature and Truth* (London: Duckworth, 1908), p. 116.

is found in Athanasius's account of the Fall, where he portrays the unfallen Adam as if he were a Platonist philosopher.[33] There is no hint of this in Genesis. S. R. Driver may be quoted at this point:

> As regards the *condition of man before the Fall*, there is a mistake not infrequently made, which it is important to correct. It is sometimes supposed that the first man was a being of developed intellectual capacity, perfect in the entire range of his faculties, a being so gifted that the greatest and ablest of those who have lived subsequently have been described as the 'rags' or 'ruins' of Adam. This view of the high intellectual capacities of our first parents has been familiarized to many by the great poem of Milton, who represents Adam and Eve as holding discourse together in words of singular elevation, refinement, and grace. But there is nothing in the representation of Genesis to justify it; and it is opposed to everything that we know of the methods of God's providence.[34]

How soon did the Fall occur? This question is not without significance in the relation between Genesis and science. If the Fall occurred at an early stage in the life of Adam and Eve we do not have to postulate an era of human history in which humanity was unfallen and which would need to be fitted into the scientific reconstruction of that history. Genesis does not tell us how soon the Fall occurred, but the exegetical tradition inclines towards the view that it happened quickly. Calvin notes that Augustine allows only six hours of unfallen history while others delay the Fall until the sabbath. Calvin, typically, avoids speculation, but concludes:

> As for myself, since I have nothing to assert positively respecting the time, so I think it may be gathered from the narration of Moses, that they did not long retain the dignity they had received; for as soon as he has said they were created, he passes, without the mention of any other thing, to their fall.[35]

---

33. Athanasius, *Contra Gentes*, ch. 2.

34. S. R. Driver, *The Book of Genesis* (London: Methuen, 1907), p. 56 (his emphasis).

35. J. Calvin, *Commentaries on the First Book of Moses called Genesis*, 2 vols. (Grand Rapids: Eerdmans, 1948 reprint), 1:156 (on Gen. 3:6).

It is wrong to state, with Barth that 'the first man was immediately the first sinner'.[36] So to conflate creation and Fall is in effect to abandon the doctrine of the Fall and thus to blame human sin on the way we were created. There is no original sin (in the sense of a fall) without a preceding original righteousness. But that preceding state need not be lengthy and, according to Christian tradition, was not. Such a brief stage of original righteousness need not conflict with the scientific account.

The above modifications of the traditional picture have been made in the interests of fidelity to the Genesis account. It will be apparent that they also lessen the tension with the scientific account. N. P. Williams was right to observe that the only account of the Fall which is tenable today is that which 'views the first human sin rather as a *praevaricatio*, a stepping-aside from the true line of upward progress, than as a *lapsus* or fall from a high level of moral and intellectual endowment'.[37] While modern science makes the latter view all but impossible, Scripture clearly favours the former view.

© A. N. S. Lane, 2009

---

36. K. Barth, *CD* IV/1, p. 508.

37. N. P. Williams, *The Ideas of the Fall and of Original Sin* (London: Longmans, Green & Co., 1927), p. 514. (Agreement with this statement of Williams does not imply approval of his reconstruction of the Fall.)

7. THE THEOLOGY OF THE FALL AND THE ORIGINS OF EVIL

Henri Blocher

If I were to choose an epigraph for this essay, it would be from Ecclesiastes: 'God made the human being upright, but they have sought many devices' (7:29b). The rare word translated as 'devices' suggests an exercise of calculating reason, a thought that implies computing procedures.[1] I hear in the verse an invitation to bring together preoccupations stamped by the rational style which reigns

---

1. The word is *ḥiššĕbônôt*, plural of *ḥiššābôn*, from the root *ḥšb*, to reckon, compute, think. It only occurs once elsewhere, in 2 Chr. 26:15, for engines of war, battering machines (technical reason at work!). It is very similar to *ḥešbôn* (same consonants), another infrequent word, found twice in the same paragraph, Eccl. 7:25a and 27b (with 'statistics' in v. 28!). A wordplay is most likely; the LXX and the Vulgate respectively use the same Greek word (*logismos*) and Latin word (*ratio*) in verses 27 and 29 to render both Hebrew terms, showing how close in meaning they were felt to be. Maybe a warning that our reasoning powers, our tool to try and fathom the deeper layers of objective reality (v. 24), are also being used to avoid what is right!

among our sciences, with the topic of humankind's loss of original righteousness.

I write as theologian and an amateur in the sciences (regarding the *status quaestionis* in the sciences of nature, although I did read several works to update my fragments of scientific knowledge). As a theologian, my confession is unabashedly *evangelical*, indeed 'conservative evangelical'. I adhere to a high view of Scripture, as the word of God written and fully trustworthy. I have no doubt that such has been the historic Christian belief. The church historian George Gordon Coulton, writing in the *Encyclopaedia Britannica* illustrates this: 'St. Thomas Aquinas had been as convinced as any later Protestant theologian that the Bible was inerrant not only in its spiritual teaching but even on matters of historical fact.'[2] Similar statements can be found from patristic times on. More: I espouse the classical Protestant discipline of hermeneutics, that readers should seek the original intention of the original author, using all the philological tools available (since the writer entered into the tacit contract of linguistic communication) and seeing her/his speech-act in its historical context – albeit avoiding sliding into historicism and the 'contextual fallacy'. Only secondarily should we reflect on the modern relevance of the meaning and any confrontation with contemporary scientific opinion.

A convenient starting point is the recent commentary by John Collins on the first chapters of Genesis,[3] because any reflection on the 'theology of the Fall' must deal with these passages. I take Collins' presuppositions to be sound, though some of his exegeses are open to criticism. In addition, we should shun a *fideistic* approach, which totally severs theological concerns from scientific data, and remain wary of a *concordistic* one, at least in stronger versions of that genre (i.e. reading modern scientific views into the biblical text). This is particularly important in dealing with the first part of the interpretative task (discerning what the inspired writer meant for the primary audience he had in mind in his own time and circumstances).

---

2. 'Reformation', *Encyclopaedia Britannica* (1961 edn), XIX, 36a.
3. John Collins, *Genesis 1–4: A Linguistic, Literary, and Theological Commentary* (Phillipsburg: P&R Publishing, 2006).

Notwithstanding, concordance may be relevant in the second part when we reflect on what the text means for us today. From this basis, this essay recalls what passes for scientific orthodoxy, sketches a critical response, and highlights the intention of the scriptural account; it reflects on the 'otherness' of evil and considers consequences; and finally investigates possible correlations or contradictions between the proposed understanding of the 'Fall' and the results of (palaeo) anthropological research as commonly understood.

The backdrop, or inevitable partner: the majority view

What is the predominant representation of the 'Fall' – the common description of what Genesis 3 recounts in narrative form, including the origins of evil? I use predominant in the sense of that which predominates in the academic world. This can be regarded as a microcosm (*mikrokosmos*) and to a great extent a *dokēsikosmos*, that is a world built of appearances and opinions (*dokēsis*), and hence something which often evades the rough encounter with the real.[4] In this arena, preferences should not be revered as dogma, nor free critique silenced by social pressure. At the same time, majority consensus should not be despised, nor *a priori* mistrusted: it is the fruit of an enormous amount of hard work on the part of gifted researchers who interact with each another, and who, though sinners, still benefit from God's 'common grace'. There are built-in self-correcting mechanisms in the way the scientific community functions, but these do not make 'science' immune from errors, frauds or ideological slant. Nonetheless, we must, at least, give science a respectful hearing.

---

4. This is not to suggest, with Paul Feyerabend, that 'anything goes' in science, implying that the mere beliefs of the tribe of scientists represent the effective norm. While maintaining the ideal of objective knowledge, my remarks are intended to point to the mixture of ideological and other factors in the work of scientists, in order to 'demythologize' hasty claims to objectivity and to definitive validity (or at least exclusive validity for today), ruling other options out of court.

Two main attitudes about the Garden story in Genesis 3 prevail and mix in Academia. There are many who *play down the importance* of the chapter. It does not speak of a 'fall', they say, nor even expressly of sin. The argument goes that the story finds practically no echo in the Old Testament, and very little in the New, apart from a rather artificial use in Romans 5. James Barr makes this point strongly, although he is well answered by C. J. Collins. Augustine is the chief culprit in this dark shadow of misinterpretation, which has affected more than a thousand years of Western religion.

Others pay more attention to the story, but insist that it should be read as *myth* or *saga*, not as true history in the ordinary sense of that word. While accepting that the Genesis narrative exhibits original features compared to other specimens of a similar literary genre, the key for these interpreters is that the story must *not* be understood as referring to a particular event in space and time, dividing a chronologically prior state of sinlessness and freedom from evil from a subsequent one of sinfulness and alienation. The positive value of Genesis 3 for such people is that it pictures, through symbols, essential traits of the universal experience of evil in time and space. So, the claim goes, it is more meaningful than if it were historical.[5] Christopher Southgate's recent book, while a sensitive and moderate treatment overall, repeatedly, with overtones of anger, calls for the rejection of any idea of a historical Fall, condemning it as a 'spurious' reading.[6]

Views on evil and its origins in this 'micro-dokesi-cosm' cannot

---

5. A third attitude comes from interpreters who attempt to reverse the direction and to celebrate Gen. 3 as a 'fall upwards'; I remember listening to a brilliant exposition of this kind by the feminist Corinne Lanoir, who praised Eve's liberating role.

6. Christopher Southgate, *The Groaning of Creation: God, Evolution, and the Problem of Evil* (Louisville and London: Westminster John Knox Press, 2008), pp. 28–35 and *passim*, p. 132 for 'spurious'; note also that the 'profound wisdom' (p. 101) ascribed to Gen. 3 is bound to the proposition: 'the Fall account in Genesis reflects a general condition rather than a historical chronology.'

be brought together and synthesized sensibly into a unified understanding; they are far too divergent. On the other hand, they share
a characteristic of being little concerned with individual guilt. The
typical discourse adopts the victim's stance: the speaker sets herself
or himself up as the victim of some power or speaks on behalf of
victims.[7] One trend concentrates on *political* evil; this is the focus of
Jürgen Moltmann with his theme of 'after Auschwitz'.[8] Its origin is
sometimes ascribed to inadequacies in social structures, but more
often it is associated with *power*, regarded as evil per se. That a free,
autonomous subject should be subjected to coercive measures is
seen to be a scandal; any use of force is condemned as 'violence'.[9]

---

7. See my 'The Doctrine of Sin in a Victim-Based Culture', in Angus
   Morrison (ed.), *Tolerance and Truth: The Spirit of the Age or the Spirit of God?*
   (Edinburgh: Rutherford House, 2007), pp. 95–114.

8. Moltmann is most emphatic in his *Religion, Revolution and the Future*,
   transl. M. Douglas Meeks (New York: Charles Scribner's Sons, 1969),
   e.g. pp. 100, 219 ('the old cosmological theodicy question about evil and
   misfortune has become today a political question'), cf. p. 141f., though he
   also tackles the thought of a mixture of 'non-being' with being in the first
   creation (pp. 35, 61, 106–107, 127–128; cf. pp. 163–164 in reply to Bloch,
   p. 196), non-being which shall be eliminated at the End, a more 'metaphysical' approach. Though Moltmann later distanced himself from the
   Marxist climate of those years, they were formative for his whole theology
   and left their imprint on his way of thinking.

9. Moltmann again may be called to witness, since an 'anarchic' – though
   moderate – streak is discerned in all his work, albeit kept within reasonable bounds. Thus he consistently interprets 1 Cor. 15:24 (the overthrow
   of all principality, authority and power, of social and political authorities):
   'On earth his abolition of all earthly power in the eternal presence of
   God can be interpreted as anarchy. Human subordination and super-
   ordination, and a system of justice enforced by power, is to be replaced
   by the brotherhood of all men . . .', dominion-free (*The Church in the
   Power of the Spirit: A Contribution to Messianic Ecclesiology*, transl. Margaret
   Kohl, [London: SCM, 1977], p. 104). As Andreas J. Beck stresses, 'Die
   postmoderne Christologie Jürgen Moltmanns. Darstellung und biblisch-
   theologische Kritik, ihre Voraussetzungen und Implikationen,

Another wide consensus among intellectuals and 'opinion-makers' is that what is *really* evil about evil is *pain*; factors which cause suffering or entail or inflict pain are regarded only as derivatively evil. Thinkers from the natural sciences usually approach the problem of evil as inevitable in evolution, involving pain in the struggle for life and the extinction of species. Indeed there are some who show real concern about the catastrophe which wiped out the dinosaurs 65 million years ago (Christopher Southgate highlights the fact that 98% of all species have disappeared through evolution.[10]) Some insist on the disorder and waste that evolution entails. Evil in human behaviour is often interpreted as a relic of past evolution, an anachronistic residue causing dysfunction.

To deal with evil thus approached, many thinkers offer some sort of a theodicy ('justifications of God'), developed along three main lines, with various combinations:

Footnote 9 (*cont.*)

> *Fundamentum* (1994/3), p. 90, 'the real sin of humankind is *Gewalttätigkeit*' (*Der Weg Jesu Christi*, pp. 148f): *Gewalt/tätigkeit* would mean, etymologically, 'power-activity', but it is the common word for 'violence' and Moltmann takes pains on the same pages to distinguish between violence and power (he does not advocate strict non-violence). Many readers, I suspect, have no inkling that Jacques Ellul was much less cautious and argued at length, on biblical grounds, in favour of anarchy in his article 'Anarchie et christianisme', *Contrepoint* 15 (1974), pp. 157–173 (p. 172: the Christian hope in politics is the destruction of power); statements are also found in his books, e.g. *Autopsie de la revolution* (Paris: Calmann-Lévy, 1969), p. 316, 'Bakounin is perfectly right. . .'; *Si tu es le Fils de Dieu: Souffrances et tentations de Jésus* (Paris: Centurion and Zurich: BV R. Brockhaus, 1991), p. 18 ('A good magistrate does not exist, domination *is* corruption'); p. 76 (all governments emanate from Satan); p. 96 (Jesus never uses constraint). I offer these references as telling and perhaps unexpected illustrations, rather than to document the sweeping summaries I am making. This is an ambition beyond this presentation. Of course, the assimilation of evil and power is typical of post-structuralist, post-Michel Foucault, 'deconstructionism'.

10. Southgate, *Groaning of Creation*, p. 15.

- *The constraints of the case:* the way things have been and worked together was the 'only way' God could wisely choose if he wanted to create. This 'free-will defence' is applied to the creation of humankind (which is part of the evolutionary process) – God had to take the risk of human beings choosing badly in order to make possible a free response of loving obedience.
- *On balance:* the good outweighs all the evils implied in *creation/evolution*;[11] to reach this optimistic conclusion, some rely on dialectics and trust the 'fecundity' of the negative.
- *God so human:* God cannot be accused if nature is 'red in tooth and claw' if the picture of God as almighty is discarded; God is rather the co-sufferer with his creatures. A God who shows such sympathy (and therefore draws our contemporaries' sympathy in turn) is often defined in 'panentheistic' terms ('panentheism', a word coined by Karl Christian Friedrich Krause [1781–1832], may be considered a mild and timid form of pantheism), but he can also be conceived as a finite partner in the evolving world-process.

A critical response: on biblical grounds

How may we respond in trusting obedience to the teaching of Scripture but without closing our minds; how can we remain open to the force of serious arguments soundly based on objective data?

Whatever the tensions, the non-historical interpretation of Genesis 3 is no option for a *consistent* Christian believer (of course, many are happily inconsistent here, as we all are, to some extent, somewhere). It conflicts openly with Paul's comments in Romans

---

11. When Richard Swinburne, the courageous theist philosopher, feels compelled to argue in *The Existence of God* (Oxford: Clarendon Press, ²2004) p. 241, that to find a good that compensates (and beyond) for pain and death in animal evolution, that sorrow for 'the victims of carnivorous dinosaurs millions of years ago is compassion for a fellow creature . . . the world is better for there being such concern'; this reader is tempted to smile.

5 – as many acknowledge who deny historicity for themselves. Christopher Southgate follows Patricia Williams who charges the apostle with 'misreading' Genesis.[12] Similar confessions, by professedly Christian scholars, such as the notable Jesuit Gustave Martelet, amount to the same definite disagreement.[13] It is impossible to minimize its import: Paul's reference to Adam in Romans 5, the *one man* contrasted with the many, is no mere homiletical embellishment: it belongs to a careful *a fortiori* demonstration ('how much more' indicates the logical structure of the chapter, vv. 9–10, 15, 17). It is impossible to treat Romans 5 as an isolated, and so presumably erratic, fragment in the Pauline corpus; the Adam/Christ parallel and echoes of Genesis 1 – 3 are recurring elements.[14] Likewise, it is not possible to drive a wedge between Paul and the rest of the New Testament. Although using different conceptual schemes, the Johannine corpus also shows a keen interest in the Eden narrative, as in the references to the Devil as a liar and murderer from the beginning (John 8:44), and to the 'original serpent' (Rev. 12:9; 20:2, *archarios* could be so translated), and there are significant allusions in the Synoptic Gospels. These textual facts cannot be simply dismissed by arguing they represent a 'projection' foreign to the original meaning. Not only is Second-Temple Judaism remarkably attentive to Adam and Eve's disobedience as the cause of death for all (Ecclesiasticus 25:24;

---

12. Southgate, *Groaning of Creation*, p. 29.

13. G. Martelet, *Libre Réponse à un scandale. La faute originelle, la souffrance et la mort* (Théologies; Paris: Cerf, 1986), p. 63, writes of 'the historically precarious nature of the information of both [Genesis and Paul] concerning the existence of "Adam" – they knew nothing more than we do' (actually, Martelet means that we know better: he does admit that 'we cannot doubt that the Fall narrative has in view [*vise*] biological death through sin', p. 33, but adds that Catholic exegesis has learnt, rightly, to distance itself from that way of thinking; one must avoid, 'exegetical fundamentalism' that produces 'devastating results', p. 50, and, 'pernicious' ideas, p. 49).

14. Cf. C. Marvin Pate, *The Glory of Adam and the Afflictions of the Righteous: Pauline Suffering in Context* (Lewiston: Edwin Mullen Press, 1993), which devotes nine chapters to the detailed study of relevant passages.

Wisdom 2:23f; 2 Baruch 48:42f and *passim*; 4 Ezra 4:30, 7:118f; possibly 1 QS [Qumran Hymns] 9:13 – despite Judaism's fascination with the angelic fall found in Gen. 6), but the Old Testament certainly contains echoes of the Eden story audible to a sensitive ear. The traditional (and simpler) reading of Hosea 6:7 that 'like *Adam* they violated my covenant' still finds supporters today, despite common translations of 'Adam' as 'mankind' or its emendation to 'Adamah' (i.e. a place name). Psalm 82 and Ezekiel 28 probably recalled the story to original hearers.[15] Other prophetic passages could be cited. Wisdom texts, such as Job 31:33 and 15:7–35 and the whole book of Ecclesiastes, have been interpreted as a commentary on the first chapters of Genesis.[16] On top of all this, we should add canonical pride of place: as Margaret Shuster aptly remarks: 'the story is given prominence by its very position at the beginning of the Bible.'[17]

Far from being a 'misreading,' the historical understanding fits the function of the story in its literary context, as the first of the series of *tôlēdôt*, genealogical traditions, whose series constitute the linear progress of the book of Genesis as historical.[18] It agrees with

---

15. Such a critical scholar as Howard N. Wallace acknowledges: 'The reference to, *'ādām* would certainly recall to the hearers of this psalm the fate of Adam in Gen. 2–3...' and 'Ezekiel 28 and 31 reveal a knowledge of the Eden tradition', *The Eden Narrative* (Harvard Semitic Monographs 32; Atlanta: Scholars' Press, 1985), pp. 185–186.

16. For a development of the argument and of what follows, see my *Original Sin: Illuminating the Riddle* (New Studies in Biblical Theology 5; Leicester: Apollos, 1997). I am offering here a condensed and somewhat updated version.

17. 'Sin', in *Global Dictionary of Theology*, ed. William A. Dyrness and Veli-Matti Kärkkäinen (Downers Grove and Nottingham: IVP, 2008), pp. 820–821.

18. 'History' is understood in its common, and basic, meaning: an account of things which really happened in time and space, and does not involve conformity to habits and norms of modern historiography. C. J. Collins (*Genesis*, pp. 249–251) underscores this point and specifies that it does not rule out 'figurative or imaginative elements', selectivity and 'ideological' slant, freedom with chronological sequence.

features that differ essentially from the genre of myth and legend[19] – which are slippery categories for all writers. At a deeper level, it does justice to the original *intention* of Genesis, which the liberal Protestant philosopher Paul Ricoeur discerned with rare lucidity.[20] Among all myths of origins, the 'Adamic myth' (as Ricoeur persisted in calling the Genesis narrative) is *unique* in separating the origin of being – creation, whose result is 'superlatively good' (Gen. 1:31, *mĕ'ōd*, used for the superlative, means first 'force, might') – from the origin of evil, a later intrusion. Instead of a metaphysical explanation of evil (an ingredient of being), we have an ethical-relational-historical one. Indeed, Ricoeur sees this as the only way to maintain 'ethical monotheism'. The presence of evil in the world cannot be denied but everything proceeds from a single principle, a perfectly good God. 'Evil becomes scandalous at the same time as it becomes historical.'[21] The prophetic denunciation and sin and call to repentance cannot be grounded in any other way. The issue of historicity here is no peripheral matter for hair-splitting theologians: it is vital for the biblical message – it is the heart of the message.

There are indeed similarities with the myths of the surrounding nations, but they are insufficient to cancel out the main historical thesis. This is not to deny that the Genesis story performs the aetiological function of myths – revealing the cause of present features of human experience (Why birth-pangs? Why relational difficulties between men and women? Why death in the end?), but why should anyone see this an objection against historicity? What if the *true* cause was an event that really occurred? Myth may be interpreted as the *lie* humans devised in the darkness of their ignorance, and an excuse for lack of the true answer. Traits that speak of myth – a life-giving plant, a serpent who speaks naturally (no: *the*

---

19. So the French Catholic and critical scholar Pierre Gibert, *Bible, mythes et récits de commencements* ('Parole de Dieu'; Paris: Seuil, 1986), especially pp. 91–102. (Gibert's interpretation next moves away from the simple recognition of historical value.)

20. P. Ricoeur, *The Symbolism of Evil*, transl. Emerson Buchanan (Boston: Beacon, 1964).

21. Ibid., p. 203.

Serpent) – do not determine the basic character of the narrative. On the one hand, we must remember that nothing resembles true banknotes more than counterfeit ones! On the other, significant differences outweigh any similarities. 'Just as one swallow does not make a summer, a few mythical traits do not constitute a mythical story.'[22] With James Orr, a valiant defender of biblical trustworthiness (and innovative apologist), I am ready to acknowledge the use of a pictorial-symbolic language in Genesis 2 – 3, accepting the genre 'as old tradition clothed in oriental allegorical dress', more freely than many evangelical scholars, including Collins,[23] 'but the truth embodied in that narrative, viz. the fall of man from an original state of purity, I take to be vital to the Christian view'.[24] The issue is not whether we have a historical account of the Fall, but whether we have the account of a historical Fall.

The *real* ground on which deniers of historicity stand, as several among them have honestly acknowledged, is its apparent contradiction with scientific opinion. I cannot repress the feeling that such deniers desperately try to ignore the biblical intention to affirm historicity, because of 'its complete lack of congruity with the scientific narrative of the unfolding of the biosphere'.[25] I return to this below; at this stage, I wish only to note how much

---

22. Gibert, *Bible, mythes*, p. 97.

23. Collins, *Genesis*, preserves several literal interpretations of tradition; yet, he suggests, that the forming of man and woman 'may reflect background conventions' (p. 252); he writes: 'It looks like the manner of presentation in these chapters of Genesis is deliberately in terms of the audience's experience – which means that it will hardly be surprising to find anachronism' (p. 203); he grants that Gen. 1 'actually depends on an anthropomorphic presentation' (p. 230); he introduces an interesting distinction between 'world picture' and 'worldview' (the latter being taught) (p. 261); and concludes emphatically: 'From whatever perspective we bring to the word *scientific*, it should be clear that Genesis 1:1–2:3 is not a scientific account' (p. 266). He may be more flexible than he looks at first!

24. James Orr, *The Christian View of God and the World* (Grand Rapids: Eerdmans, repr. 1960), p. 185.

25. Southgate, *Groaning of Creation*, p. 28.

fallible interpretation goes into scientific opinion-making, never mind alien psychological and sociological factors. Conjecture, even unanimously accepted and seemingly likely in the face of available evidence, remains conjecture. On the other side, mature faith is able patiently to endure unsolved conflicts.

On the problem of evil and its origin, we must proceed step by step. My comments are no more than preliminary remarks. We should begin by acknowledging the glaring inadequacy of the theodicies offered on the basis of modern opinion, particularly when we face the light of the consistent Christian (biblical) perspective. The sovereignty and transcendence of the God revealed in Scripture, high and lifted up, the King of Ages, the Blessed and Only Ruler, independently of whom not a sparrow falls to the ground and yet who dwells in inaccessible light, seems to be forgotten. The vision that is discarded is *not* the 'Greek' Platonic one, as some suggest, but simply the biblical testimony. Where in Scripture, for instance, is there any hint that God suffers when animals suffer, as Southgate believes?[26] God as the Co-Sufferer does not even provide a clear answer to the problem of *human* pain. John Rogerson has commented on a book of essays dealing with theodicy, 'An interesting conclusion of Tom Holmén's general essay on the New Testament is that it nowhere supports what in recent theology has become a standard Christian response to theodicy, namely, that God participates in human evil and suffering in order to overcome it.'[27] Whether or not one fully endorses this conclusion, the warning about groundless speculation fuelled by modern sentimentality is worth taking to heart.

We must acknowledge that the balance of good and bad is impossible to assess. Who can review all the relevant evidence? Where are the scales and measures? And the Karamazov dilemma (that no universal good will ever compensate for one child's night of anguish) remains a sting in the tail: the whole cannot compensate

---

26. Ibid., p. 50 and *passim*.

27. J. W. Rogerson, 'Review (Book of the Month) of *Theodicy in the World of the Bible*', A. Laato and J. C. de Moor (eds.), Leiden, E.J. Brill, 2003, 830 pp.,' *Expository Times* 115/12 (2004), p. 411.

for the part when the part is horrible beyond measure. Christopher Southgate faces the problem and offers the solution of resurrection and immortality for all *individual* animals, heaven for young pelicans in 'some sort of self-transcended pelicanness'.[28] Inasmuch as the status and origin of evil is concerned, these theories try to view the negative aspects of experience as part and parcel of normal reality, as natural features of the universe (progress is achieved through struggle, life arises from death, power with its destructive effects is the affirmation of value. . .). Evil is naturalized, made into an ingredient of being: a strategy wholly opposed to the unique message of Genesis.[29] Two misconceptions have to be dealt with in order to make room for a more biblical strategy. The first misapprehension is the focus on pain or suffering as capital evil. Scripture teaches otherwise. Thus for Otto A. Piper: 'Biblical thought is not primarily preoccupied with escaping suffering or with seeking pleasure, but rather with shunning sin.'[30] Attitudes and behaviour that turn away

---

28. Southgate, *Groaning of Creation*, p. 89 (and his whole ch. 5). He wavers somewhat on p. 84: 'I concede that simple organisms may possess little distinctive individual experience or agency, and they may be represented in the eschaton as types rather than individuals.' Where is the criterion? At any rate one should expect to meet not a few vigorous rats in heaven. . . He considers the idea of an 'objective immortality' in the memory of God (pp. 86–87), but he is not comfortable enough with it – and rightly so, for 'immortality' is a misnomer, a sophist's semantic fraud, since being remembered is no immortality at all.

29. One appreciates Gordon Graham's lucid comment on free-will defence, *Evil and Christian Ethics* (New Studies in Christian Ethics; Cambridge: Cambridge University Press, 2001): 'A Free Will theodicy seems to show that some evils are logically necessary, logically necessary, that is to say, to the realisation of freedom, and hence beyond the will even of God. If this is true, however, any such theodicy still faces a serious difficulty; it succeeds not so much in justifying evil, as eliminating it' (I take 'justifying evil' as elliptic for 'justifying the divine permission of evil'), p. 169–170.

30. 'Suffering and Evil', *Interpreter's Dictionary of the Bible*, vol. 4, ed. George A. Buttrick (Nashville: Abingdon, 1962), p. 451. Cf. p. 450: 'The evil character

from the Giver God, absolute Goodness as personal life, constitute capital evil, which is sin. When sin has entered the scene, other evils follow: the tyranny of alienation that makes sin a bondage (John 8:34), and the 'harvest' of deserved punishments – the evils that befall human beings and are experienced as antagonistic to their lives. To maintain such an insight, as will be seen, it is necessary to deny the true evilness of happenings that are considered evil by many. The second error is that not all which passes for evil should be so categorized in biblical perspective. A cool-headed examination of the data must take place.

Sharpening analysis: the otherness of evil

The intention of the unique pattern set forth by Genesis 1 – 3 (and in chapters 4 and 11) is to highlight the *otherness* of evil. 'Sin is an anomaly,' Cornelius Plantinga Jr writes, 'an intruder, a notorious gate-crasher. Sin does not belong in God's world, but somehow it has gotten in.'[31] This alien character must be explored further if the Genesis 3 'Fall' and the origin of evil is to be seen in the light of revelation.

The otherness of evil implies the failure of rational theodicies that purport to account for evil by finding it a place within the system. Evil as evil is that which cannot be *comprehended* – that is, taken-with-the-rest; it must be preached against and fought against as an alien intruder. It is the *atopon* itself,[32] and finding a place for it amounts to 'explaining away' its evilness, which is but a short step to excusing it. When disorder is 'solved' into superior order, it is dissolved. This is the case in predominantly monistic systems, such

---

Footnote 30 (*cont.*)
>   of the happenings and conditions is not seen . . . in their being obstacles to man's desire for happiness, but rather in their rendering faith difficult.'
31. Cornelius Plantinga Jr, *Not The Way It's Supposed to Be: A Breviary of Sin* (Grand Rapids: Eerdmans and Leicester: Apollos, 1995), p. 88.
32. *Atopos* means 'that has no place' (*topos*), but it is used in Greek as a strong word of moral disapproval, 'wrong, improper', as in Polycarp's Epistle to the Philippians 5:3 (*ta atopa*), and for men in 2 Thess. 3:2.

as Plotinus' or Leibniz', and in dualism; symmetry, after all, offers a *beautiful* reduction to order. It is also the case, paradoxically, in nihilistic pluralism, irrationalistic philosophies of ultimate disorder. They only *appear* to take evil seriously: if disorder is the rule, how can one speak of disorder any more? (Of course, nobody can speak any more. . .) Indignation and shame vanish, as representing super-nonsense among bubbles of nonsense. And this is why the *sovereign* God of Scripture requires evil be named and denounced as evil.

It must be emphasized that the otherness of evil is not the same as any other otherness. There is a good otherness that distinguishes creatures from one another, within the beautifully ordered multi-plicity of God's works. Sin and the consequences of sin are parasitic on this harmony and destructive of it. It is even too weak to say that evil otherness is *sui generis*, as Gerrit C. Berkouwer has done with the worthy intention of stressing the same point,[33] because there is no kind (or *genus*) to which evil can belong in the sense that there are *genera* instituted in creation! This mad, foul, vile otherness, the uncanniest uncanny, can only be approached in thought through purely abstract definition – that which is contrary to God's will of precept and of desire (the reflection of God's character) – or, to use Plato's phrase for the *chōra* (the receptacle of 'forms' whose resistance explains evil in the sensible world), 'by a kind of bastard reasoning',[34] through the metaphors of corruption and perversion.

Since human reason is intended to promote harmony, since it incorporates the impulse to unify, the temptation to 'explain' the otherness of evil in the way of created otherness is ever present. Even worthy evangelical scholars come perilously close to making chaotic otherness part of original being, often on the basis of a seductive reading of Job.[35] In order to ward off the temptation, we

33. Gerrit C. Berkouwer, *Sin*, transl. Philip C. Holtrop (Studies in Dogmatics; Grand Rapids: Eerdmans, 1971), p. 141.

34. *Timaeus* 52B (*logismo; tini nothô;*).

35. Bruce K. Waltke, *An Old Testament Theology: An Exegetical, Canonical, and Thematic Approach* (Grand Rapids: Zondervan, 2007): 'Somehow, in God's design, there is, within the boundaries of the cosmos, chaotic energy . . . hostile to life' (p. 12), ; 'These paradoxes show that evil is part of God's 'order'

must handle the tricky notion of the *possible* with care; I am afraid tradition has been insufficiently vigilant. Sin entered the world through the misuse of their freedom by Adam and Eve; how logical it sounds to infer that sin (evil) was *possible* at the previous stage! But is it legitimate to apply *logic* here? It is legitimate to infer A (created possibility) from B (actuality); but evil is an alien discontinuity. Unthinkingly applying the logic of inference to 'evil B' (and thus affirming [A] the possibility of evil, as involved in freedom, or in finiteness) amounts to *surreptitiously* denying the otherness of evil by 'naturalizing' it and giving it some kind of footing within the order of being. Against this common procedure, the position here advocated could be summarized as insisting that evil was *not impossible* in the state of original innocence, which is not equivalent to saying that it was 'possible' – if by 'possibility' we do not mean only the mere abstract notion (non-good) but a *real* possibility (in Kierkegaard's phrase), one aspect of created freedom that already helps us understand how evil became actual.[36]

Drawing out implications: contrary to widespread feeling

The otherness of evil as historical intrusion, with no footing in God's superlatively good creation, can only be maintained

---

Footnote 35 *(cont.)*

> (p. 939); also pp. 941, 127 on chaos in Gen. 1:2 – despite the denial of chaos (*tōhû*) in Isa. 45:18. Robert S. Fyall's doctoral dissertation (*Now My Eyes Have Seen You: Images of Creation and Evil in the Book of Job*, New Studies in Biblical Theology 12; Leicester: Apollos and Downers Grove, IVP, 2002) puts to use a highly impressive Near-Eastern erudition (especially Ugaritic) and many stimulating insights to buttress the thesis that 'sinister powers' are 'rooted in creation': he sees a 'sinister abyss' in Gen. 1 (p. 149), 'where a lurking menace is in some way embodied in creation itself' (p. 134); he remains ambiguous, however, since he adds sentences speaking of *fallen* creation, and also includes the argument of autonomous free-will (pp. 144, 189).

36. Karl Barth, *CD*, IV/1, p. 409–410, within his own framework discerned the trap in the usual talk about the possibility of sin involved in freedom.

(consistently) if one resists some common assumptions. What some label 'metaphysical evil', meaning being subject to limitations or lacking the fullness of being which is God's ('imperfection' may be used), is obviously no evil if all evil is restricted to sin and the consequences of sin. This restriction removes the acuteness of evil, since in judging evil, the fact of being limited in any way (like humankind not having an elephant's strength or eyes all around the head) will appear to most an arbitrary decision. The problem of 'physical evil', if one chooses so to speak, is not solved so easily. We need to examine the relevance of cosmic processes that damage human lives, such as earthquakes and germs, and – a serious concern for authors like Southgate – what befalls animals along the evolutionary road.

Some 'solutions' are certainly blind alleys. The idea that animal death and catastrophic events, earthquakes or tsunamis, are consequences of Adam's disobedience or are part of the havoc brought by the previous fall of 'Lucifer' (a suggestion put forward by Alvin Plantinga), lack all scriptural warrant. Indeed, several passages praise the wisdom of God *the Creator* as they describe the way carnivorous animals participate in the food chain (e.g. Pss. 104; 147; Job 38 – 41). Nowhere does the Bible describe the Fall as a kind of second creation with power to establish a new *order* for life in the universe – for it can hardly be denied that the phenomena of which we speak are part of a functioning order in the universe. Southgate discards this pseudo-solution,[37] while Collins remarks: 'Nowhere does it [the text] imply that somehow human sin has distorted the workings of the natural elements.'[38] He adds an argument that should prove effective with extreme literalists: many animals live in *water* and are carnivorous (whereas the curse in Genesis 3 affects the earth)[39] although he probably goes too far when he severs all links between Genesis 3:16 and the groaning of Romans 8 (he refers 'corruption' or 'decay' to Genesis 6:11–13).[40]

---

37. Southgate, *Groaning of Creation*, p. 28.

38. Collins, *Genesis*, p. 164.

39. Ibid., p. 165.

40. Ibid., p. 183.

Indeed, Romans 8 does not support any theory about animal death resulting from human sin: the bondage to futility and decay is not defined (a few interpreters restrict 'creation' in Romans 8 to humankind, but this is unlikely).

As already suggested, the attempt to show that advantages outweigh inconveniences appears too questionable to 'justify' animal death and the other phenomena, even if they must be considered as evil. Southgate is right when he concludes that the good of the species cannot compensate enough for the fate of the individual victim.[41]

One way of dealing with evil is simply to deny that the phenomena deserve to be counted as evil. The method exemplified by Alexander the Great is appropriate here. Instead of trying to untie the famous Gordian knot, he cut the knot! Before the phenomena that some consider 'evil', I simply want to deny that they deserve to be counted as evil. It is not so difficult! Earthquakes, volcano eruptions, germs, viruses are not considered evil *in themselves* in Scripture: they express the power of God (as at Sinai), sent as messages of his holiness and embodying the wisdom of his untraceable ways (Job 38). As is well-known, most germs do little harm to a healthy body – one can easily presume that in the full health of original integrity, the immune system of the man and the woman would counter any potentially harmful disturbance. Similarly, humans would enjoy enough strength, and wisdom and possible powers of premonition (as even today some animals possess) to avert all negative consequences of earthquakes, etc. Such a hypothesis finds the *locus* of the evil consequences of sin in the *relationship* between humankind and nature, as set out in Genesis 3 (and Rom. 8 may be read in that light; see also Rev. 11:18). It also implies that unfallen goodness encounters a proper degree of resistance on the part of nature – hence the mandate subdue (Gen. 1:28) and work (2:15) – which humankind was able joyfully to overcome: paradise does not mean dreamland like the mythical Cockaigne, but an environment suited to human fulfilment.

Biblical perspectives on carnivory are hardly compatible with an

---

41. Southgate, *Groaning of Creation*, pp. 44–47.

'evil' assessment of animal death. Why should it be so tarnished? The classical Epicurean arguments against the fear of death are relevant here: atoms that were combined for a time now part company – so what? Epicurean reasoning has cogency for animals, although it must be rejected in the case of human death because of the human difference, the transcendence of the *imago Dei*, that implies eternity in the heart (Eccl. 3:11). The death of animals that are our close companions make us sad, but this is a subjective projection and must be kept within bounds. The philosopher Peter T. Geach wisely remarks that 'someone who tried to sympathize with a shark or octopus or herring would be erring by excess as Dr Moreau erred by defect; their life is too alien to ours for sympathy to be anything but folly or affectation'.[42] A similar denial applies to Southgate's preoccupation with species extinction as a major evil. Why consider it so? Why demand that a species, once created, should exist eternally? Why not acknowledge that it is a sign – indeed a perfection – of God's ordering that this segment of cosmological time was assigned to that particular species?

I confess I find *animal pain or suffering* much more difficult to handle.[43] Even if animal death fits the harmony of cosmic processes, is not pain, anguish and ferocity evil? Here are a few thoughts that may be helpful:

- Apparently, the problem has only been one to the last few generations, and mostly for Westerners; Hindu reverence for life belongs to another framework altogether. Are we better than our forefathers? Is our late-modern sensitivity a reliable guide? Could it be that our feelings (so strong in this matter) have been unduly fashioned by the *Zeitgeist* (or failure of *Geist*)?

---

42. Peter T. Geach, *Providence and Evil* (Cambridge: Cambridge University Press, 1977), p. 80.

43. Some writers distinguish between the two words, so R. F. Hurding, 'Suffering', *New Dictionary of Christian Ethics and Pastoral Theology*, ed. David J. Atkinson and David H. Field (Leicester and Downers Grove: IVP, 1995), p. 823. My dictionaries show such an overlap between the two semantic ranges that I will use the two words as roughly synonymous.

- There is no trace in Scripture of a serious concern about this aspect of animal life. 'Does God bother about oxen?' (1 Cor. 9:9). Animal mores serve as symbols, on the basis of human projections onto animals near to us, nothing more distinct.
- Just as with animal death, animal pain touches us most with animals that are our companions. Where do we draw the line? If someone feels moral concern for the 'suffering' of rats, flies or lice, Geach's strictures sound relevant. Some theologians sound as if ridicule never killed anyone.
- A crucial point was made by C. S. Lewis, long ago. Although Southgate uncritically attributes 'selves' to animals,[44] it is reasonable to doubt that even higher animals are *selves* in a meaningful sense of the word.[45] None can say 'I'. Even the fact that some animals, including elephants and the great apes (but not gorillas) recognize their own image in a mirror does not amount to the constitution of a *self*.[46] And if there is no self to suffer, the problem of suffering is set in very different terms.

The problem of animal pain will probably remain without a solution as long as the *metaphysical* (and *theological*) enigma of animal life and its powers remain unelucidated. My suggestion is not that humanity can be interpreted on the basis of animal life, but the reverse: humanity, in God's design, should be the starting-point, and beasts understood as fashioned and endowed to be our nearest companions among earthly creatures.

---

44. Southgate, *Groaning of Creation*, p. 42 and passim.
45. C. S. Lewis, *The Problem of Pain* (London: Geoffrey Bles, Centenary Press, 1940), ch 9.
46. See the conclusion of Pascal Picq, in Pascal Picq and Yves Coppens (eds.), *Aux origines de l'humanité, II: Le propre de l'homme* (Paris: Fayard, 2002), p. 517, referring especially to a chapter by Boris Cyrulnik: though he obviously wishes to minimize the animal/human difference (against what he calls 'humanisme intégriste'), Picq has to acknowledge a qualitative discontinuity. One may add that on the point whether great apes are able to understand the mental states of other individuals, scientists disagree among themselves.

Confronting palaeoanthropology: mature faith endures uncertainties

Once the divine voice has been heard through the human witnesses of inspired Scripture, it is appropriate that we should test our biblical interpretation against the views of those who investigate the 'natural' field, dig out *vestigia* of the past and reconstruct the story. Such views may prompt us to go back to our Bibles to check our exegesis; alternatively, they may reinforce some of our conclusions or perhaps produce tensions that must be borne patiently.

Some results of biblical research may stand as assured and reduce the likelihood of direct contact (conflict or confirmation) with scientific theories: the pictorial character of the Garden narrative and its account of the origin of evil; the import of the Genesis 5 genealogies – are still enigmatic for me.[47] The tragic events of the aboriginal apostasy as Adam and Eve asserted themselves as autonomous, 'like gods', are told in a language more suited to the revelation of *meaning* than to inform us on precise date and location, or the particular form of the disobedience. Hence, biblically-informed faith has no a priori need to discard representations of human origins quite different from those current prior to 1700 or even 1850 AD.

A historical Fall is a non-negotiable article of faith. However the record of *Homo sapiens'* early history does not provide any specific confirmation of such a transition between righteous and blessed fellowship with God and the reign of sin and death. Is this a serious problem? The data which might present some degree of relevance are few and meagre. Jacques Cauvin discerns a major break in religious consciousness at the beginning of the Neolithic age, with an explosion of idolatry, especially anthropomorphic idolatry, and violence among humans.[48] Edgar Morin, nearer to

47. Collins, *Genesis*, pp. 202–207, shows they cannot be used, additionally, to date Adam or Cain.
48. According to Jean-Denis Vigne, interviewed by Muriel Valin, *Science et Vie* 235, special issue (June 2006), p. 131.

consensus, eloquently describes how *Homo sapiens*, at least since the cultural breakthrough 40,000 years ago, deserves the name *Homo demens*; with *sapiens-demens*, error and illusion, *hubris*, violence, magic and gods avid for sacrifices, fill the space of the world to be conquered.[49] The lack of *vestigia* from an 'Edenic' state, however, should not surprise and embarrass believers. Even if that state was enjoyed for some time (years and not hours as some have thought), the chances of finding convincing traces are practically nil. The absence of proof is no proof of absence.

Clearly this is not the whole story. We cannot escape confrontation with palaeoanthropology over the identification of the biblical Adam. 'Adam, where art thou?' In the present state of knowledge, Adam is hard to locate in the prehistorians' schemes. Fixed reference-points there are: the unity of present humankind, called 'modern man' or *Homo sapiens*, must be affirmed biblically (Acts 17: 26); scientific opinion concurs, though parameters and interests differ. This humankind, the *běnê 'ādām* in biblical parlance, constitutes 'theological' *Homo*, God's living image, made for covenant and fellowship with him, with powers that transcend biology. Here at least is a convergence with the scientific recognition of the unique cultural abilities and achievements of *Homo sapiens*: the mastery of double-articulation language, the symbolic inventions and multi-layered reflective consciousness. Collins reminds us that attempts to deny human difference 'typically founder on closer inspection' and quotes from Susan Milius: 'None of our models of reciprocity [among nonhuman animals] can accommodate the psychology of human friendship.'[50] The general law of 'threshold effect' may account for a fact that should

---

49. Edgar Morin, *Le Paradigme perdu: la nature humaine* (Points 109; Paris: Seuil, rev. edn 1979), pp. 123–124, 142–145, 162; on error and *hubris*, pp. 118–123 ; on religion, p. 159, etc. Morin's idea lies far from that of a 'fall': on the contrary, he sees all the fury and destructive drives as the ransom of the human powers, the two being twin entailments of 'hyper-complexity'.

50. Collins, *Genesis*, p. 257, with n. 13 (S. Milius' article 'Beast Buddies,' *Science News* 164/18 [2003], pp. 282–284).

not count as an objection; the presence of similar traits in higher animals remain below threshold and do not confer 'theologically human' status.

But when? If one accepts the dates and patterns suggested by palaeoanthropology, three timings seem possible for Adam, none of them free from difficulty. A Neolithic Adam would be most attractive if one considers Genesis 4, which looks 'Neolithic' indeed. But this proposal requires abandoning Adam's fatherhood of all present humans (the ancestors of present populations were scattered on the various continents long before the Neolithic age). Such a wise and pious scholar as Derek Kidner thought it was permissible,[51] with the privilege of the divine image conferred to other humans under Adam's federal headship; yet, the tension with the 'natural sense' of Scripture is hard to bear. Furthermore, this solution would exclude from theological humankind the tremendous artists of the Cro-Magnon population, with the masterful paintings of the Grotte Chauvet (dated 32,000 BC), near Vallon Pont-d'Arc in Ardèche. Emmanuel Anati has convincingly analyzed this work, showing how the syntax of the drawings reflect a complex logic and a 'sophisticated ideology', 'a truly philosophical vision of existence', with unmistakable religious beliefs.[52]

Twenty years ago, it looked as if the entire *sapiens sapiens* population could have proceeded from one centre around c. 40,000 BC. Adam could be located there and then, as father as well as 'head' – tentatively. But this is no longer the case. The fossils of 'modern' *sapiens* found in the Carmel finds (Qafzeh and Skhul) have been dated c. 95,000 BC by several independent methods.[53]

---

51. Derek Kidner, *Genesis* (TOTC; London: Inter-Varsity Press, 1967), pp. 28–30.

52. 'Les Premiers Arts sur la terre,' in Picq and Coppens (eds.), *Aux origines de l'humanité, I: De l'apparition de la vie à l'homme moderne* (Paris: Fayard, 2002), pp. 510–559 (with an additional piece by P. Picq, pp. 560–565), with phrases taken from pp. 512, 529, 553. The study is not based on a small selection – there are 40,000 millions images of art known in the world, or fragments, coming from prehistorical times (pp. 558–559).

53. Bernard Vandermeersch, 'L'Origine des hommes modernes', in *Aux*

Experts disagree as to the way *Homo sapiens* populated the globe, but DNA studies tend to show that the dispersion of ancestors was accomplished long before 40,000 BC.[54] The genetic fatherhood of Adam does not seem to be compatible with that timing, though all previous remains (artefacts, suggestion of burial rites, including among Neanderthals) seem below the theological threshold. The third solution is incapable of proof as well as of disproof: it places Adam well before 100,000 BC. The low level of cultural achievements during the many subsequent millennia can then be interpreted as the effect of degeneracy; no decisive scientific or exegetical objection (we know so little about the intention of the genealogies anyway) can be raised – but who can deny the frustration of our intellectual imagination and sensitivity?

We should not be embarrassed to conclude with uncertainty: it is a mark of a mature faith, properly based on adequate evidence and serenely bearing the tensions of a pilgrim's progress by faith, not sight. Free from a neurotic need for certainty on every matter, we trust the trustworthy Creator and Redeemer.

© Henri Blocher, 2009

Footnote 53 (*cont.*)
    origines I, pp. 416–463, esp. 432. Cf. Eric Crubézy and José Braga, 'Aux origines d'*Homo sapiens*', *Les Dossiers de la Recherche* 32 (2008), p. 71.
54. Roberto Macchiarelli, 'Par où sont-ils sortis d'Afrique?' ibid., p.66.

8. BLOCHER, ORIGINAL SIN AND EVOLUTION

Richard Mortimer

Henri Blocher is probably best known for his book *In the Beginning: The Opening Chapters of Genesis*[1] (*ITB*). In this he expounds the first three chapters of Genesis (with a pointer to the chapters that follow). The book has been widely read and its contribution has been significant, having a moderating effect in creation/evolution debates. Where this debate is so often marked by open hostility and a caricaturing of the 'enemy', Blocher's work points us back to Scripture and to the realization that, rightly understood, Scripture and science stand more closely together than is sometimes thought.

Blocher's *Original Sin: Illuminating the Riddle*[2] (*OS*) is perhaps less well known but is marked by the same fair-mindedness and exegetical thoroughness. It is based upon a series of lectures delivered at Moore College, Sydney, Australia in 1995. It represents a careful account of the doctrine of original sin founded on Scripture and is

---

1. H. Blocher, *In the Beginning: The Opening Chapters of Genesis* (Leicester: IVP, 1984).
2. H. Blocher, *Original Sin: Illuminating the Riddle* (Leicester: Apollos, 1997).

sensitive both to human experience and to the debates of modern theology and science. In his preface to the book, Don Carson describes Henri Blocher as 'a theologian of the very first rank, and still too little known outside the francophone world'.[3] Such praise is justified in that few writers combine so well a rigorous and informed commitment to the primacy of Scripture and a breadth of knowledge of the wider theological debates.

Why is his work important? To state the problem baldly, the doctrine of original sin, to judge by its critics, lacks biblical warrant, is incoherent, unscientific and unhelpful! In the face of such an onslaught Blocher reasserts not only the scriptural validity of the doctrine but also its positive value.

To assess the value of Blocher's contribution to the subject of original sin, we first offer an overview of his position, drawing chiefly on *OS* (but with reference to other writings, as appropriate). We then look more fully at the challenge of the evolutionary perspective and some of the alternative responses to be found. We conclude with a critical evaluation; what are Blocher's most valuable insights and what areas require further questioning and exploration?

Original sin

The question of method and defining the doctrine
The essence of Blocher's approach is clear: 'Sound theological method requires that we listen to Scripture as a whole, according to the analogy of the faith.'[4] Thus he follows Reformation principles. But he also recognizes the importance of science and this comes to the fore in *ITB*. He seeks to employ science in his theological enterprise by giving it what he terms a '*ministerial*, servant

---

3. *OS*, p. 7.

4. *OS*, p. 17. Blocher elucidates the principle in 'The "Analogy of the Faith" in the Study of Scripture', in N. de S. Cameron (ed.), *The Challenge of Evangelical Theology: Essays in Approach and Method* (Edinburgh: Rutherford House, 1987).

role'.[5] He is keen to preserve the principle of *sola Scriptura* but recognizes that biblical interpretation includes bringing our own knowledge to the text:

> In fact no interpretation can develop in a vacuum; all interpretation appeals to the services of prior knowledge. In order to understand a text one uses one's knowledge not only of the language but also of the reality encompassed by the word (the referent).[6]

So what rule should be applied to the application of scientific theory in the task of interpretation?

> We suggest the following: we have the right to bring our prior knowledge of reality to bear only as far as we can presuppose it in the *human* author of the biblical text . . . That rule follows from the humanity of Holy Scripture. In the act of inspiration God did not turn his spokesmen into robots; his word became their word, under their signature and responsibility. Thus we have no right to go over their heads in order to set forth a 'divine' meaning which they would never possibly have imagined – even if those men did not grasp the whole import of what they attested (1 Pet. 1:10ff).[7]

We find a similar line maintained by Blocher in *OS*. As a preliminary to some observations about palaeoanthropology, he writes:

> Faithfully obeying the *sola Scriptura* rule, the 'formal principle' of the Reformers, Christians dare refuse modern scientific knowledge a *constitutive* role in the interpretation of biblical texts; but a fideistic

---

5. *ITB*, p. 25, emphasis his.

6. Ibid.

7. *ITB*, p. 26. Bernard Ramm makes a similar observation: '*The theological and eternal truths of the Bible are in and through the human and the cultural . . .* The biblical statements about Nature are non-postulational or phenomenal' (*The Christian View of Science and Scripture* [London: Paternoster, 1955], p. 244, emphasis his). This summarizes an earlier section where he explores biblical language and a biblical view of nature (pp. 45–69).

separation between science and faith betrays the biblical sense of truth. Once instructed by the sovereign word of God, our faith welcomes whatever information, drawn from God's 'general revelation', holds proper credentials.[8]

We see below (in particular under 'Genesis 3') how this works out in practice.

In OS, having affirmed the primacy of Scripture, Blocher still has to give a working definition of the doctrine which is to be the subject of his scriptural analysis and further reflections. Drawing on Calvin,[9] he identifies four aspects to the doctrine of original sin: human sinfulness is universal, it has become part of human nature itself, it is inherited and it stems from Adam. He argues briefly, but incisively, how Scripture both supports, and qualifies, these assertions.[10] The two foundational texts of Genesis 3 and Romans 5 are then singled out for individual attention, permitting the space to explore them in further detail and allowing Blocher to develop his own distinctive emphases, as we see below.

Genesis 3

For Blocher, the challenge of evolution is but one of several that confront an Augustinian understanding of Genesis 3. Another challenge, surprisingly perhaps, comes from biblical scholarship. Many scholars see Adam as a marginal figure within the biblical scheme (the Pauline corpus excepted). Theology, likewise, presents a challenge in that sinfulness is often viewed not as having a beginning, as such, but as simply being an abiding aspect of the human condition. Each of these issues is examined by Blocher.

Palaeoanthropology

Blocher takes the scientific consensus seriously. So, when it comes to interpreting the opening chapters of Genesis, he is prepared to

---

8. OS, p. 39.

9. Whose views he recognizes as standing in the Augustinian tradition (OS, pp. 17, 19).

10. This is the subject of OS, ch. 1, pp. 15–35.

embrace scientific theories – where the text permits. In the case of the days of creation (which is critical to *ITB*) the poetic and schematic nature of the text suggests an assertion of divine order, a 'literary'[11] rather than a literal description of physical processes. To some extent the same pertains to the Eden narrative of Genesis 2:4 – 3:24, although here the matter is more complicated. Blocher recognizes in the text characteristics associated with wisdom literature,[12] and can speak of 'a dream like garden'[13] but he also argues that the genealogies, in particular, are intended to establish Adam and Eve's historical rootedness.[14]

This last point assumes great importance, for, as we see below (in 'The Fall as an event'), Blocher argues that it is of the essence of the narrative that there was an historical entrance of sin into the human experience. Where might such an event fit within the palaeoanthropological data? Following J. Davis, Blocher argues that the story of Cain and Abel fits well with what we know about neolithic farming communities. The genealogical link to Adam and Eve may be viewed as describing descent on a selective basis, rather than comprehensively detailing the full lineage. Accordingly, it is possible to view Adam and Eve as a pair of Cro-Magnons, c. 40,000 BC, from whom all today's human stock might have originated. On this basis Blocher resolves the tension between the scientific and biblical accounts.[15]

Now, Blocher sounds a cautious note towards science. He notes that in seeking harmony we should not become slaves to the latest theory, recognizing that any theory may be revised in the light of

---

11. *ITB*, p. 49.

12. *ITB*, p. 36, with reference to L. Alonso-Schlökel, 'Sapiential and Covenant Themes in Genesis 2–3', in J. Crenshaw (ed.), *Studies in Ancient Israelite Wisdom* (New York: KTAV Publishing House, 1976), pp. 468–480.

13. *ITB*, p. 35.

14. *ITB*, p. 162.

15. *OS*, pp. 40–42, and also the French second edition of *ITB*: *Révélation des origines: Le début de la Genèse* (Lausanne: Presses Bibliques Universitaires, 1988), p. 254, citing J. Davis, 'Genesis, Inerrancy and the Antiquity of Man', in R. Nicole and J. Ramsay Michaels (eds.), *Inerrancy and Common Sense* (Grand Rapids: Baker Book House, 1980), pp. 137–159.

further discoveries.[16] While there is truth in that, we must, none-theless, take seriously current scientific opinion and ask whether the proposal is satisfactory in scientific terms. This is a matter to which we return in 'The evolutionary challenge', below.

Biblical intertextuality

A second challenge to the Augustinian tradition of biblical inter-pretation is that it reads into the Bible the perspective that Israel's history is portrayed as being tainted by its Adamic past, when in fact the Eden story is simply not referred to.[17] This view is summa-rized by Ricoeur, whom Blocher quotes: 'In every way the addition [of Adam] is belated and, in certain respects, non-essential . . . The prophets ignore him . . . Jesus himself never refers to the Adamic story.' In similar vein, the story is further described by Ricoeur as 'only a flying buttress', 'only a false column'.[18]

Blocher, however, rebuts the argument:

> . . . frequency of occurrence could not be the sole measure of
> importance; its place in the canon is significant. It is obvious that the
> Eden story is no peripheral anecdote or marginal addition; it belongs
> decisively to the structure of Genesis and to that of the Torah.

Drawing on Scharbert,[19] he goes on to show how the Eden story

---

16. *OS*, p. 40; *ITB*, pp. 213, 230–231.

17. E.g. G. von Rad, *Genesis* (London: SCM, rev. edn 1972), p. 102; C. Westermann, *Genesis 1–11* (London: SPCK, 1984), p. 276.

18. P. Ricoeur, *The Symbolism of Evil* (Boston: Beacon Press, 1967), pp. 237–239, cited in *OS*, p. 32. Some thirty years earlier N. P. Williams drew a similar architectural analogy, describing the Eden story (as well as the traditions associated with Gen. 6:1–4) as 'quasi-historical façades, success-fully attached to a conceptual structure which stands upon a psychological basis' (*The Ideas of the Fall and of Original Sin* [London: Longmans Green and Co. Ltd., 1927], pp. 33–34). Ricoeur may have borrowed this image; that he is influenced by Williams is evident from a reference in *Symbolism*, p. 332.

19. J. Scharbert, *Prolegomena eines Alttestamentlers zur Erbsündenlehre* (Freiburg-Basel-Vineena: Herder, 1968), cited in *OS*, p. 33.

serves an important aetiological function and that 'echoes' of it are to be found throughout Scripture. This is an important point and one for which further recent support can be adduced. In relation to the Old Testament, Stordalen's comprehensive analysis, *Echoes of Eden*, has changed the landscape. His conclusion warrants our attention:

> Despite the common view of Genesis 2–3 as 'marginal', there appeared a significant number of passages either referring to, alluding to or displaying potential similarities to the Eden story. Open references to Eden were found in similes, metaphors and allegories. Less overt references were gleaned from other allegories, allusions and potential intertexts to Genesis 2–3. In this material 'Eden' emerged as a conventional literary topic in biblical Hebrew literature – at least from the Early Persian Age onwards.[20]

In relation to the New Testament, Paul Minear's *Christians and the New Creation*[21] similarly reasserts the place of the Eden story in the imagination of the original audience. We may also, in this regard, cite N. T. Wright, who stresses the importance of Israel's story as a shared framework among the New Testament writers; for Wright that story is, 'the story of Israel understood as the story through which the creator God is restoring the creation, and with it the race of Adam and Eve'.[22]

The Fall as an event
For Brunner it is not only that science has removed Adam from the historical plane[23] but also that the intrinsic weakness of the inher-

---

20. T. Stordalen, *Echoes of Eden: Genesis 2–3 and Symbolism of the Eden Garden in Biblical Hebrew Literature* (Leuven: Peeters, 2000), p. 474.

21. P. Minear, *Christians and the New Creation, Genesis Motifs in the New Testament* (Louisville: Westminster John Knox Press, 1994).

22. N. T. Wright, *The New Testament and the People of God* (London: SPCK, 1992), p. 407.

23. To quote, 'For our generation, the fact that this narrative is no longer historically credible means that the convincing power of this impos-ing doctrine . . . has completely disappeared' (E. Brunner, *Man in Revolt* [London: Lutterworth, 1939], p. 120).

ited doctrine of original sin has now come to light. He writes, 'It is not for scientific reasons, in the main, that the historical form of the doctrine of the Fall is questionable, but for religious reasons; it has led to serious distortions of the faith, of the understanding of sin and of man's responsibility in the sight of God.'[24] In what way, we may ask? Because the schema 'emphasizes the necessity of sin at the expense of responsibility'.[25] Instead Brunner offers the view that 'the creation and the fall both lie behind the historical visible actuality, as their presuppositions which are always present'.[26] This view is shared by other twentieth-century theologians, notably Reinhold Niebuhr[27] and Ricoeur.[28] Against this Blocher reasserts the importance of an historical beginning to sin. He writes:

> Reinhold Niebuhr's emphasis on 'responsibility despite inevitability', and Ricoeur's on the rational symbol of the power of evil 'already there' in our experience of freedom, offer little more than words in praise of paradox to offset the greater likelihood of the metaphysical interpretation. That interpretation leads to the conclusion that humans

---

24. Ibid.
25. Brunner, *Man in Revolt*, p. 121.
26. Alsford helpfully describes this type of response as treating original sin as a 'tensive symbol'. It serves to express (rather than explain) the dialect of necessity with responsibility (we are slaves to sin and yet are responsible for our sin). S. Alsford, *Sin as a Problem of Twentieth Century Systematic Theology*, unpublished PhD dissertation, University of Durham, 1987.
27. Reinhold Niebuhr, *The Nature and Destiny of Man* (London: Nisbet & Co. Ltd., 1941), p. 262.
28. Ricoeur writes, for example, 'Therefore the possibility arises of interpreting the two states of innocence and sin no longer as successive, but as superimposed . . . The myth puts in succession that which is contemporaneous and cannot not be contemporaneous . . . in telling of the fall as an event it furnishes anthropology with a key concept: the *contingency* of that radical evil which the penitent is always on the point of calling his evil nature' (*Symbolism*, p. 251, his emphasis). (The problem, as Blocher argues, is that by making them simultaneous the contingency is lost.)

are evil 'as if' they had fallen; but if they did not *really* fall, they must be evil from creation and by creation.[29]

His point is that without a beginning of sin, *within history*, human sinfulness has to be a part of our created nature. Of Ricoeur he further notes, 'After contrasting the intention of the Genesis story and the tragic myth (evil ultimately rooted in the divine), he considers that "the tragic is *invincible*".'[30]

Blocher writes as one who sat under Ricoeur and has studied his work extensively. An interview puts a personal perspective on this:

I have invested much in the study and understanding of the theology and philosophy of Paul Ricoeur. I followed one of his courses for a year and I decided that he would be the one great contemporary thinker I would try to know – not exhaustively, but more than the others . . . He stressed to me what is a very important element: the contrast between a metaphysical understanding of sin, of human alienation, and the Christian understanding which is historical not metaphysical. He is the man, especially in his earlier writing on the symbolism of evil, who has understood that this is the original feature of the biblical account of evil, and that it is entirely bound to moral monotheism and the prophetic call to repentance – that these three are bound together. Although he has realised all this and said it so well, still he does not maintain the historicity himself.[31]

In *Evil and the Cross*[32] (*EC*), the underlying metaphysics of evil is given a full discussion by Blocher. The book is structured around three philosophical solutions to the problem of evil. The first

---

29. *OS*, p. 59, citing Brunner, *Man in Revolt*, pp. 399, 142, 172, 193 and Niebuhr, *Nature and Destiny*, vol. 1, pp. 255ff. In this connection Mathewes, too, observes that 'Niebuhr's metaphysical pessimism is rooted proximately in the fact that he has "naturalized" sin' (C. Mathewes, *Evil and the Augustinian Tradition* [Cambridge: CUP, 2001], p. 126).

30. *OS*, p. 61, citing Ricoeur, *Symbolism*, p. 327, emphasis Ricoeur's.

31. S. Gathercole, 'Simon Gathercole Meets Henri Blocher', *Themelios* 29:3 (2004), p. 39.

32. H. Blocher, *Evil and the Cross* (Leicester: Apollos, 1994).

is that evil is a privation and has its place in God's overall good scheme. The second, that evil arises from the misuse of freedom. The third is more abstruse – the dialectical response, found in Hegel, Barth and others – in which evil is real but 'plays a positive role . . . because it must be denied in its turn, and thus reality is set in motion, and being escapes from the deadness of a fixed condition and experiences progress'.[33]

All three views fail to take seriously the full weight of the Bible's own dialectic – the abhorrence of evil to God and the total sovereignty of God over evil. How does Blocher reconcile these apparently contradictory affirmations? The simple answer is he doesn't, he acknowledges that at the heart is an 'inscrutable mystery'.[34] While this mystery cannot be solved in theory, it *is* solved in reality, and that by the cross. The cross, for Blocher, is God's means of victory. He writes:

> The free sacrifice, unique and once for all, is the reverse of the illustration of the fruitfulness of the Negation in a universal chain of logic. At the cross evil is conquered *as evil*: corruption, perversion, disorder, a parasite, and yet also weighed down with the load of the people it has led astray and deep in debt from the responsibility incurred.[35]

It is in this light we see Blocher's objection to Barth's description of evil as *das Nichtige*. His language is forceful: '. . . we must nevertheless deplore his [Barth's] drift towards a pseudo-rational gnosis of evil. For him, evil is metaphysically *necessary*: how could such an utterance not call forth our deepest indignation?'[36]

---

33. *EC*, p. 66.
34. Ibid., p. 128.
35. Ibid., p. 132, emphasis mine.
36. Ibid., p. 82, his emphasis. We note that in interview Blocher refers to Barth as another great influence upon him and that he 'fought with Barth's theology as a young man'. He explains the issue: 'There, the key question of worldview appeared to me entirely basic: the creation fall redemption scheme, rather than the Barthian christocentric concentration' (Gathercole, 'Blocher', p. 40).

So Blocher affirms the historical schema of creation, fall and redemption. It is the historical fall that is remedied by the historical cross.[37]

Romans 5

Romans 5:12–21 is widely recognized as the 'seat' of the doctrine of original sin; the critical passage of Scripture where the link between Adam, the human race and Christ is articulated. Interpretations vary and we will not rehearse the range of opinions here. But Blocher does, tentatively, offer a distinctive perspective which we shall note.

He takes his cue from the reference to the law and Moses (vv. 13–14) which otherwise seems out of place in the passage. Perhaps these verses indicate an alternative to the dichotomy that we are either condemned for our own sin *or* for Adam's sin. Maybe instead the passage is saying that we are condemned *on the basis of* the 'covenant' between God and Adam and our standing with him. To quote:

> Today we tend to take condemnation for our own sins as a matter of simple logic. But verse 13b (*cf.* 4:15) shows that this was not the case for Paul's acute theologico-juridical mind. Without a law, sin is undefined, *apeiron*; it cannot be made the object of judgment. My hypothesis, then, is as follows: I submit that the role of Adam and of his sin in Romans 5 is *to make possible the imputation, the juridical treatment, of human sins*. His role thus brings about the condemnation of all, and its sequel death.

> If persons are considered individually, they have no standing with God, no relationship to his judgment. They are, as it were, floating in a vacuum. Sin cannot be imputed. But God sees them in Adam and through Adam, in a framework of the covenant of creation. Therefore

---

37. Further discussion by Blocher of Barth's treatment of the temporal sequence is to be found in the section '4. Human Existence in Time' (pp. 123–128), in his essay 'Karl Barth's Anthropology', in S. Chung, (ed.), *Karl Barth and Evangelical Theology: Convergences and Divergences* (Bletchley: Paternoster, 2006), pp. 96–135.

he sees their sins as committed against the Genesis 2 command, as grafted on to Adam's sin in Eden.[38]

On this basis v. 12 may be paraphrased, as follows:

> Just as through one man, Adam, sin entered the world and the sin-death connection was established, and so death could be inflicted on all as the penalty of their sins. . .[39]

Blocher does not insist on this interpretation but offers it tentatively as a constructive contribution. In the same spirit we commend this reading for wider consideration. It affords two advantages, one exegetical and one theological. Firstly, the tangential reference to Moses makes more sense with this reading. Secondly, the imputation of alien guilt need not be asserted on this view. Blocher finds this advantageous when he examines original sin from the perspective of human experience and the question of how it is propagated. To these we now turn.

The experience and propagation of original sin

Blocher cites approvingly Niebuhr's oft-quoted dictum: 'The doctrine of original sin is the only empirically verifiable doctrine of the Christian faith.' (Although he questions whether it is really the *only* one.)[40] The doctrine captures well the dualities of human existence; that we are the most noble and most wretched of God's creatures, capable of acts of great charity and creativity and equally of despicable acts of brutality.

Against the idea that human evil is but a residual from animal descent he observes that it is the very finest aspects of human nature that have the capacity to generate the vilest outcomes.[41]

---

38. *OS*, p. 77.
39. Ibid., p. 78.
40. Ibid., p. 84, citing Reinhold Niebuhr, *Man's Nature and His Communities* (New York: Scribner's, 1965), pp. 24.
41. A recent article in *The Psychologist* underlines this point. It highlights studies of the Nazi period that go beyond the idea that mass-murderers were

Indeed the being 'spiritual' as opposed to 'carnal' is no safeguard since the human spirit itself can be misdirected.[42]

So at an experiential level the doctrine of original sin, for Blocher, expresses well the riddle of human existence. The question arises whether any more can be said. Is original sin a descriptive term only, or can we fathom its causes and develop it as an explanatory tool? Whereas Berkouwer sees original sin as being beyond human comprehension (and indeed sees explaining sin as a risky enterprise, on the grounds that, 'every "explanation" of guilt in the history of theology, must lead to a self-excuse'[43]), Blocher sees such a conclusion as hasty. He agrees that we can never fathom *why* Adam sinned – to do that is, indeed, to rationalize and excuse sin. But we should be able to explain how, once it entered the world, sin has spread to all with '[u]niversality, constancy and necessity'.[44] This is required both to make the doctrine intelligible and, more particularly, to provide an account that avoids the need to view sin as a metaphysical given.

How, then, does Blocher account for sin's dominion? Blocher maintains that many of the explanatory metaphors offered are treated too literalistically or simplistically[45] and that any 'solution' needs to give proper weight to the genuine complexity of the human constitution. We are both biological and spiritual, individuals and members of one race, free and yet determined, responsible and yet slaves.

---

simply obeying orders: '[I]ndividuals needed to display *imagination* and *initiative* in order to interpret the command they were given . . . Nazis didn't obey Hitler, they worked *towards* him, seeking to surpass each other in their efforts' (A. Haslam and S. Reicher, 'Questioning the banality of evil', *The Psychologist* 21:1 [2008], p. 17).

42. *OS*, p. 87.

43. G. Berkouwer, *Sin* (Grand Rapids: Eerdmanns, 1971), p. 523.

44. *OS*, p. 109.

45. For example, sin may be viewed as being like a disease that spreads, but taking the metaphor too literally loses the dimension of human responsibility (*OS*, pp. 110–111).

The solution he offers therefore is composite. He rejects the imputation of alien guilt as being counter-intuitive and lacking biblical warrant. Similarly he rejects a 'realistic' view that sees all humanity as a single entity in Adam. Rather he sees Adam as the federal head of humankind standing in connection to humanity as the original parent. As sin is propagated from one generation to the next so, by God's creation covenant with Adam, each generation stands condemned. Sin is propagated not by a single means but by the interaction of various factors. These include cultural heredity (which operates deep in the psyche through factors such as parenting), genetics (Blocher rejects a simplistic notion of a 'sin gene' but questions, 'could there be a far more subtle disorder of the genetic formula and of its expression, a disorder which would correlate to spiritual deformation?'[46]), satanic influence and privation of righteousness.[47]

While privation is often associated with a Catholic view of original sin, Blocher finds it used by Jonathan Edwards and sees it as a key component:

> The mere deprivation of God's fellowship in foetal life, I suggest would already be enough severely to disturb the construction of personality. Jonathan Edwards . . . strongly insisted on the effect of the mere removal of original graces: 'Only God's withdrawing, . . . and his [man's] *natural* principle's being *left to themselves* is sufficient to account for his becoming entirely corrupt and bent on sinning against God.'

Blocher's account is nuanced and multi-faceted and avoids the traps of more simplistic solutions. It presents, we suggest, a persuasive account of a biblical understanding of original sin. Nonetheless the evolutionary worldview offers a very different way of looking at things, one that would challenge Blocher's standpoint. To what extent do his views withstand that challenge? It is to that question we now turn.

---

46. *OS*, p. 125.
47. Ibid., pp. 122–128.

The evolutionary challenge

Two areas of evolutionary research pose problems to Blocher's synthesis. The first is palaeoanthropology and the second sociobiology. The former casts doubt on the credibility of Adam as the progenitor of humankind and the second challenges original sin as a concept for interpreting human behaviour, replacing it with evolved instincts. We consider these in turn.

Monogenism?

Blocher defends the view that Adam and Eve were a literal couple from whom the human race derives. The technical term for this view is 'monogenism'.[48] While Blocher's scientific sources persuade him that this is a viable option, the general consensus is that the founding group must have consisted of many individuals. Humans developed, it is believed, over a period of time in East Africa[49] and then spread from there into other areas of the globe. Studies of mitochondrial DNA, which is passed entirely down the female

---

48. Other relevant terms are polyphyletism (that humans evolved in several lines in many and various places) and monophyletism (a single line from a particular region) (see *OS*, p. 40, n. 11). These terms are further explained in K. Rahner, 'Monogenism', in *Sacramentum Mundi*, vol. 4 (London: Burns & Oates, 1968), pp. 105–107 and A. Kasujja, *Polygenism and the Theology of Original Sin Today* (Rome: Urbaniana University Press, 1986), pp. 21–22.

49. There is little dispute that *Homo sapiens* is derived from a single stock. In the preceding chapter of this book, Blocher maintains his interpretation that this was represented by a single couple. He acknowledges that the scientific consensus is moving towards an early date for the origin of *H. sapiens*, but maintains that the science is necessarily provisional and that theology should not change to accommodate uncertain science. In ch. 2 of this volume, Berry argues that this problem disappears when we take the view that the making of humans-in-the-image-of-God is not a genetic event detectable by physical anthropology and hence can be dated more recently without conflicting with palaeoanthropological understanding (see p. 61).

line, and of the male-determining Y-chromosome, suggests that this took place some 150,000–200,000 years ago[50] (see ch. 2 of this volume, p. 57). Allan Day comments, '. . . it can be asserted that the chance of "mitochondrial Eve" mating with the common male antecedent is so small that it is virtually non existent.'[51] Of course genetics is a subject still in development[52] and some conclusions may change, but there is, we maintain, a need to respond to this information.

One response to this is to reassert a federal view of Adam.[53] Recent proponents such as Kidner and Spanner present this as an alternative to direct parentage.[54] This suffers from two problems, however. Firstly, it undermines the unity of humankind, since we are no longer all Adam's descendants (cf. Act 17:26). Secondly it fails to offer a mechanism for the spread of both God's image and the power of sin over the human race, which under traditional federal theology coincided with biological descent.[55] Indeed

---

50. A. Day, 'Adam, Anthropology and the Genesis Record', *Science and Christian Belief* 10.2 (1998), p. 131. Forster and Marston helpfully set out the alternatives diagrammatically (R. Forster and P. Marston, *Reason, Science and Faith* [Crowborough: Monarch Books, 1999], p. 436).

51. Day, 'Adam', p. 131.

52. W. Gibbs, 'The Unseen Genome: Gems Among the Junk', *Scientific American* (2003), pp. 26–33, illustrates major new areas of discovery regarding genetic material beyond protein coding genes.

53. From the Latin *foedus*, meaning 'covenant'. In its classic form, federal theology, such as that propounded by its seventeenth-century Dutch exponent, Johannes Cocceius, proposed two covenants by which God related to humankind, the first an Adamic covenant of works and the second a covenant of grace, through Christ. (See M. Watts's introduction to T. Boston, *A View of the Covenant of Grace* [Lewes: Focus Christian Ministries, 1990], for useful background.)

54. D. Kidner, *Genesis* (London: IVP, 1967), pp. 28–31 and D. Spanner, *Biblical Creation and the Theory of Evolution* (Exeter: Paternoster, 1987), pp. 76–80, 107–114.

55. For some critical observations see Day, 'Adam', pp. 136–137. That lineage and representation were traditionally held together is indicated by Murray:

Blocher's solution combines a federal view with biological descent because on its own the imputation of guilt, under the federal scheme, sits uneasily with a 'biblically formed' sense of personal responsibility.[56]

Another approach is to see the figures of Adam and Eve as representing a population rather than a couple. This approach preserves the unity of humankind, since we really are the descendants of a single population. (Indeed, more generally within biology, genes are carried within populations; a species that has only one member – at least if it reproduces sexually – is, in effect, an extinct species!) This view pictures sin as spreading within the first population and hence to all humankind. Rahner offers this solution. He makes the following important point early on in his argument:

> It is a general principle of biology that true, *concrete*, genetic unity is not found in the individual but in the population within which alone many individuals can exist . . .[57]

He continues:

> Therefore *mankind remains a biological-historical unity, even in terms of polygenism,* because of the real unity (i.e., based on real factors and not a process of abstraction) of physical existence . . . because of the real unity of the animal population from which mankind descended . . . because of the real unity of the concrete biotope[58] . . . because of the actual human and personal intercommunication, which, in any case, is not merely a

---

'[I]t may not be unnecessary to repeat that the representative view does not deny but rather affirms the natural headship of Adam, the seminal union of Adam and posterity. . .' (J. Murray, *The Imputation of Adam's Sin*, Phillipsburg: Presbyterian and Reformed Publishing Co., 1959, p. 37). Blocher also cites Turretin in this regard (*OS*, p. 117).

56. *OS*, 74.

57. K. Rahner, 'Evolution and Original Sin', *Concilium: Church and World* III.6.3 (1967), p. 32.

58. 'Biotope' he defines as an 'area in which the main environmental conditions and biotypes adapted to them are uniform' (Rahner, 'Evolution', p. 32).

result but a constitutive element of the biological and *historical* unity of mankind as such . . . [and] finally because of the unity of man's destiny towards a supernatural aim and Christ. . .[59]

The position needs to be developed[60] but, in principle, it offers a way of viewing the fall of Adam and Eve as *historical* while accepting polygenism.[61]

Sociobiology

Sociobiology may be defined as 'the study of social behaviour in animals and humans, esp. in relation to its survival value and evolutionary origins'.[62] The question arises whether the phenomenon explained by Blocher in terms of original sin can better be explained with reference to evolution. Such a comparison, however, cannot be made directly since biology cannot speak of sin as such; it is a theological term that takes God to be its point of reference.

To advance our discussion, therefore, we shall look at sociobiology through a theological lens and, for this purpose, compare Blocher's conservative interpretation of original sin with that of Patricia Williams in her book *Doing Without Adam and Eve: Sociobiology and Original Sin*.[63] Embracing the insights and claims of

---

59. Ibid., pp. 32–33.

60. For example was there a single first sin or is it possible for sin to 'grow' in a group setting alongside the growth in human potential? (See A. Dubarle, *The Biblical Doctrine of Original Sin* [New York: Herder and Herder, 1964], pp. 226, 236–237.) Could the image of God, often thought of as bestowed on Adam, be thought of as applying to a population, perhaps typified by Adam, Eve and Seth? (See J. Moltmann, *God in Creation* [London: SCM, 1985], pp. 234–243, and in particular the reference to Gregory of Nazianzus, p. 235.) Or could the federal and polygenistic perspectives be combined by viewing Adam as a tribal leader *within* an evolving population?

61. Day, 'Adam', pp. 138–141 also argues along these lines, recognizing a corporate and an individual meaning for 'Adam'.

62. Collins English Dictionary (6th edn., 2003).

63. P. Williams, *Doing Without Adam and Eve: Sociobiology and Original Sin* (Minneapolis: Fortress Press, 2001).

sociobiology in a wholesale manner she is concerned to recast the Christian metanarrative accordingly. An extended dialogue with her treatment is instructive.

Williams develops her approach with devastating honesty. For her, literalists are at fault in upholding a belief in an originating human pair, but so too are liberals in describing humankind as 'alienated'. She writes:

> Science says the claim liberal theology has retained from literalism, that we are alienated and exiled, is false.[64] Humanity evolved here on Earth. This is our native habitation. The elements in our bodies originate in the stars that light our way home. Our blood comes from the salt seas that stroke our shores. We are related to all other organisms . . . We know how to live here and have done so with remarkable success.[65]

For Williams, sociobiology presents the human condition in a complex but, overall, positive light:

---

64. We note here recent works that accuse 'secular' philosophers, namely, Freud, Nietzsche, Heidegger and Wittgenstein as unwittingly absorbing and perpetuating the myth of the fall: R. Webster, *Why Freud Was Wrong: Sin, Science and Psychoanalysis* (London: HarperCollins, rev. edn 1996) and S. Mulhall, *Philosophical Myths of the Fall* (Princeton: Princeton University Press, 2005). While Mulhall hints at the possible value of the religious perspective of the fall tradition, Webster wants to remove it. He writes, for example, '. . .Freud's "scientific" enterprise followed almost exactly the same pattern as many earlier attempts to revive the doctrine of Original Sin. Freud no less than Swift or Wesley, offered a view of the personality which saw human nature as radically divided against itself. The animal impulses and appetites which he located in the self were characterised in predominantly negative terms. The most obscene levels of the sexual imagination were not, according to Freud, to be affirmed or incorporated into the whole identity and liberated as part of the riches of the self. Rather they were to be intellectually acknowledged and then controlled and sublimated through the power of reason' (Webster, *Freud*, p. 318).

65. Williams, *Doing Without Adam*, p. 199–200.

Sociobiology tells us we are remarkably flexible and free. It tells us our self-interest is a natural product of evolution without which we would fail to flourish, but self-interest also leads us into fear and egocentricity Sociobiology tells us we naturally love our kin . . . but it may also involve us in nepotism, murder and genocide. Indeed, we have too many conflicting desires and too many choices. When we make wrong ones, evil comes into our lives.[66]

On this basis, Jesus did not die to atone for our sin, but gave us teachings and lived, and died, to show us how to live as God's creatures in God's world, beloved and accepted by him and, furthermore, he gives his presence to help and transform us. Together, then, the teachings of Jesus and the teachings of science can revitalize Christianity:

> Because science has a model of human nature to substitute for that
> in the Christian doctrine of original sin, it finally enables Christianity
> to turn away from Adam and Eve and come face to face with Jesus.
> When Christian theology searches for truth rather than assuming it
> knows the truth, when it accepts the demise of Adam and Eve and
> discovers human nature, instead, in sociobiology, when it turns to Jesus
> to learn how to manage our remarkably complex nature, Christianity
> will heed Jesus' message and also embrace the unification of science and
> Christianity.[67]

Williams's revisionism should not be dismissed lightly; she is not, we suggest, pioneering an eccentric view from the margins. Rather, she is responding to a shift in outlook that has substantially already happened in Western culture. Human nature is seen neither as fatally corrupted, nor deeply alienated, nor even (in the terms of Romanticism) as naturally good – it is simply a quirky

---

66. Willams, ibid., p. 200. Midgley similarly sees the human situation as one of responding to competing drives and making moral choices (M. Midgley, *The Ethical Primate: Humans, Freedom and Morality* [London: Routledge, 1994], pp. 177–184).
67. Willams, *Doing Without Adam*, p. 201.

ragbag to be lived with, enjoyed, and patched up when things go wrong.[68]

But things do go wrong, and indeed Williams acknowledges this:

> We stuff ourselves with sweets, swill alcohol, and gamble our homes
> away. The desires themselves are natural enough. A species whose
> ancestors' diet was rich in fruit inherited the desire for sweet tastes that
> led its ancestors to food then steered them between the unripe and
> the rotten; natural opiates in our brains help control pain; weighing
> and taking risks is part of daily life. But we live in a world far different
> from that of our ancestors, a world where candy racks line supermarket
> checkouts, liquor is available in the corner store, and gambling
> establishments dot the land.[69]

Elsewhere she refers to sin as 'part of our nature', and even describes how the presence of the risen Christ, 'helps us overcome our evolved bondage to sin and death'.[70] What Williams declines to do, however, is to connect the endemic problem of evolved sin to the Eden story, preferring instead to do away with Adam and Eve altogether and stressing, instead, God's abiding forgiveness and Jesus' capacity to transform us.

Now, while Williams's analysis is widely divergent from

---

68. Witness 'blank irony' as a feature of postmodernity (N. Mercer,
    'Postmodernity and Rationality: the Final Credits or Just a Commercial
    Break?', in A. Billington, A. Lane and M. Turner (eds.), *Mission and
    Meaning, Essays Presented to Peter Cotterell* [Carlisle: Paternoster, 1995],
    p. 329), or the demise of 'sin-talk' (A. McFadyen, *Bound to Sin: Abuse,
    Holocaust and the Christian Doctrine of Sin* [Cambridge: CUP, 2000],
    pp. 1–13), or the loss of import of moral dialogue (A. MacIntyre, *After
    Virtue – A Study in Moral Theory* [London: Duckworth, 1981]), or the popu-
    larity of philosophical works concerned with practical wisdom for living
    rather than metaphysics or epistemology (notably, A. de Botton, *The
    Consolations of Philosophy* [London: Penguin, 2000]).
69. Williams, *Doing Without Adam*, p. 149.
70. Ibid., pp. 186, 198.

Blocher's we see also that there are points of contact, as, for example, with the recognition that people can become enslaved to their appetites. Also both see 'privation of righteousness' as a helpful concept in so far as it corresponds to the difficulty humans have in balancing their conflicting desires.[71] This is a key point since it highlights the limits of sociobiology alone. In so far as we are determined by our instincts sociobiology adequately accounts for human behaviour. But once we entertain making informed choices between our instincts we enter another realm. This is admitted for example by Richard Dawkins in *The Selfish Gene*. Having argued that we are both produced and controlled by survival-driven replicators (genes) he concludes on an optimistic note: 'We, alone on earth, can rebel against the tyranny of the selfish replicators.'[72] Here he affirms what our intuition tells us, that the will chooses between our instincts. And it is precisely the capacity to exercise the will rightly that has been lost, according to the doctrine of original sin.

While Williams and Blocher both see humans as lacking the ability to rightly balance their appetites, where they radically disagree[73] is that Blocher insists that privation makes us guilty. Not that alien guilt is imputed but that even as we grow our will develops wrongly and our intentions mark us as guilty.[74] Hence Blocher sees atonement as the central work of salvation[75] and Williams denies this.[76] Which view reflects the reality of the situation more

71. *OS*, pp. 127–128, 130; Williams, *Doing Without Adam*, pp. 55–62, 148–152. Williams is drawn to Athanasius's account, although, of course, she rejects a historical Adam.

72. Richard Dawkins, *The Selfish Gene* (Oxford: OUP, ²1989), p. 201. In the first edition (1976) this was the closing sentence. It evoked some comment, to which Dawkins replies in the endnotes of second edition (pp. 331–332).

73. And with regard to the historicity of Adam and Eve, which we considered above.

74. *OS*, pp. 128–129, 134.

75. Ibid., p. 132.

76. Williams, *Doing Without Adam*, pp. 197–198. More precisely she redefines atonement: 'This new interpretation of at-one-ment rejects the doctrine

fully? Both give account for our desire to sin but Blocher makes a surer case for why we exercise our will in favour of those desires. Moreover Blocher's account takes seriously the enormity of the problem of sin in the biblical schema. In contrast, Williams's dismissal of the theological need for sacrifice makes light of the problem and diminishes the sense the holiness of God.

Evaluation and conclusion

Blocher's contribution, we maintain, has to be set against the wider scene in which the 'classic' understanding of original sin is attacked as lacking biblical warrant, incoherent, unscientific and unhelpful. We have seen that Blocher argues convincingly for a biblical understanding of original sin and makes some helpful new suggestions in understanding Romans 5. He further offers an account of original sin that does not violate an intuitive and biblically informed sense of justice. In so doing he demonstrates the coherence and positive value of the doctrine. Regarding science, Blocher's approach affirms a harmony between science and Scripture. This assertion bears scrutiny methodologically and in relation to the issue of sociobiology. With regard to the specific issue of the origin of mankind from a single pair, we found Blocher's position to be inadequate.

Over and above all this a particular contribution of Blocher's warrants highlighting. He insists that sin entered the world in history, by human choice, and not as a necessary element within the created order. Sin is an *historical* and not a *metaphysical* reality. This basic insight preserves theology from compromising the holiness of God. It also gives grounds for hope. For if sin is a necessary component of creation it cannot be remedied; if it is a feature of history it can. We may be guilty sinners but we are not so by design, and, by God's saving purposes, we will not be so in eternity. We leave the last word to Blocher, and his concluding remarks from *Evil and the Cross*:

---

of the atonement as an action Jesus performs so that God becomes able to forgive us. Rather Jesus' words and deeds show us that God is always forgiving us' (p. 198).

Such is the glory of the cross that one would be tempted to explain
the permission of evil *by this end*, that love, put to the test, reveals itself
in its ultimate intensity. One last time, we must resist the attraction
of the pseudo-rational Gnosticism; it would attribute to a holy God
a calculating mind which would utterly appal him. We have no other
position than at the foot of the cross. After we have been there we are
given the answer of the wisdom of God, which incenses the advocates
of optimistic theodicies or of tragic theodicies. God's answer is evil
turned back upon itself, conquered by the ultimate degree of love in the
fulfilment of justice.

This answer consoles us and summons us. It allows us to wait for the
coming of the crucified conqueror. He will wipe away the tears from
every face, *soon*.[77]

© Richard Mortimer, 2009

---

77. *EC*, pp. 133.

EPILOGUE: THE SEA OF FAITH: DARWIN DIDN'T DRAIN IT

R. J. Berry and T. A. Noble

> Darwin's ideas, while confirmed by mountains of evidence, remain startling in their implications for pre-scientific modes of thinking. They are consequently an enduring target for movements that disdain critical enquiry and the life of the mind.
>
> Leader in *The Times*, 26 December 2008

Whither have the contributors to this book brought us? We believe they have established three critical principles:

- An insistence that as new information emerges, Scripture, whilst God-given and authoritative, must be re-examined and may require reinterpreting. Christians of a former age had no doubts that the sun moves round the earth and supported their ideas from the Bible (e.g. Pss. 19:4–6; 96:10); nowadays we unhesitatingly interpret the passages which seemed to speak of a fixed earth in other ways.
- An awareness of the compelling genetic and fossil evidence that human beings have descended from an ape-like line, and that we are therefore related to other living beings.

- The uniqueness of human beings as the only creatures made in God's image, albeit 'fallen' so that life in fellowship with God is now only possible because of Christ's redeeming and reconciling death.

Putting together these three beliefs, we find ourselves in a position which seems almost impossibly conservative but also surprisingly radical: one where we accept that there must have been a 'Fall' in time and that we cannot rule out the existence of a historic Adam. We come to this position from a simple exegetical and apparently non-controversial recognition: that we are created in God's image, and that this unique relationship to the one infinite Triune God distinguishes us from the rest of creation. That act of creation was a divine and sovereign act, not a genetic mutation or the result of a 'natural' evolutionary process (even if it would have appeared so to a hypothetical observer).[1] Because of the widespread rejection of humanity's relationship to God, we affirm the historic Christian understanding that mankind disobeyed its maker and hence 'inherited the wind'. To say that we are made in the image of God is not to say that the divine image is 'in us' in such a way as to imply that we are advocating some sort of Hellenic body-soul dualism. We are not: we affirm that we are body-souls, transformed from our animal ancestry by the creating work of God. Genesis 2:7 gives some indication of this divine act by speaking of a two-stage emergence of humankind, although it would be wrong to infer that God's *rûaḥ* breathed into already existing matter was some sort of special material.

Our understanding of humanness saves us on the one hand from the contortions of ultra-conservative expositors who are

---

1. 'God's words [in Gen 1:27] affirm the creation of the human family in relation to himself, as his counterpart, so that the nature of humanity derives from the human family's relatedness to God. The concept of the *imago Dei* is fundamentally relational or covenantal . . . The distinguishing mark of human existence when compared with other creatures is thus the whole of human existence (and not some "part" of the individual)' (Joel Green, *Body, Soul, and Human Life* [Milton Keynes: Paternoster, 2008], p. 63).

forced to deny or qualify our animal ancestry and on the other, the selective readings forced on more liberal theologians. We affirm, as Paul proclaimed in Athens, '[God] created from one stock every nation of men to inhabit the whole earth's surface' (Acts 17:26); we are one because we alone are 'in God's image', not because of our membership of the species *Homo sapiens*. More importantly, we are enabled to accept the natural meaning of Paul's detailed comparison in Romans 5:12–19 and 1 Corinthians 15:45–49 between Adam and his sin and Jesus and his salvation. We can join in Paul's admonition to 'instruct certain people to give up . . . devoting themselves to interminable myths and genealogies, which give rise to mere speculation and do not further God's plan for us, which works through faith' (1 Tim. 1:3–4).[2] After all, what are 'interminable myths and genealogies' but disputes about anthropology and evolution? They divert us from a proper focus on Christ and his work.[3] As George Murphy puts it,

The standard of genuine humanity is not the biblical description of the first man and woman. If that were so, we would know almost nothing about what kind of persons we are to be. Even less is our standard to be

2. All Bible quotations in the Epilogue are REB.
3. A useful review which takes a very similar position to ours is by George Murphy, 'Roads to Paradise and Perdition: Christ, Evolution, and Original Sin' (*Perspectives on Science and Faith,* 58 [2006], pp. 109–118). Murphy begins: 'Our questions should be dealt with in the context of a theology of the Crucified One. This may seem surprising because Christians have often understood the Incarnation only as God's "Plan B" to solve the problem of sin . . . The question of whether the Incarnation would have occurred had humanity not sinned has been debated for centuries. Some medieval theologians (including Aquinas) said "No" and others "Yes". Ep. 1:10 which speaks of God's "plan for the fullness of time, to gather up all things in him [Christ], things in heaven and things on earth", favors the latter response. In modern times, Barth argued forcefully that the Incarnation is the purpose of creation . . . Our picture of creation is not one of static perfection but of divine activity in the dynamic universe, which the physical and biological sciences disclose to us' (pp. 109–110).

whatever science tells us about some early members of the genus *Homo*. The exemplar of humanity, the true image of God (Col 1:15) is Jesus Christ as he is proclaimed to us in Scripture, and God's purpose for all of us is to grow into maturity in him (Eph 4:11–16).[4]

This does not mean that we can ignore evolution and the implications of Darwinism. These have challenged us to rethink our interpretation of Scripture just as surely as Copernican cosmology did in the sixteenth and seventeenth centuries. It has implications for the way we interpret the creation narrative in Genesis 1, although it does not affect the Christian *doctrine* of creation, that God created the heavens and the earth *ex nihilo*. Despite Humanist propaganda from Huxley to Dawkins and Dennet, there is nothing in Darwin, nor in contemporary cosmology, to make us surrender that basic conviction of the faith. But Darwin's revolutionary thinking in biology has particular implications too for our understanding of Genesis 3, the narrative of the Fall and for the connected doctrine of original sin, as well as for our understanding of the creation of the universe and of the human race.

It is important that we do not rush too quickly to conflate the narrative of human origins and Fall in Genesis and the narrative of human origins given by modern science. Each discipline must be allowed its own integrity, Christian doctrine proceeding from the interpretation of Holy Scripture and science from the interpretation of empirical evidence. But our best hypothesis about human moral experience and sin might run something like this. Our prehuman ancestors cannot be called immoral (let alone 'sinful') on the grounds that they killed, deceived, behaved promiscuously, and so on. But when God created the first humans, apes now in God's image, or *Homo divinus* as John Stott has called them,[5] these creatures, since they were now brought into this unique relationship to God, became moral agents. Although they shared many inherited – including behavioural – traits with their ancestors and

---

4. Ibid., n. 3, p. 110.
5. J. R. W. Stott, *Understanding the Bible* (London: Scripture Union, 1972), p. 63.

animal relatives, this did not mean that they were dependent on or determined by them.[6] Sociobiologists fall into the naturalistic fallacy when they argue that human ethical norms are no more than correlates of our evolutionary history.[7] But the new relationship to God, being in his image, which led to new moral possibilities and responsibilities, was followed by a failure to believe and obey God, and consequently a failure to grow into the spiritual and moral greatness we were meant to exemplify. George Murphy asks us to imagine these first human beings like this:

> These humans are at the beginning of a road along which God wants
> to lead them and their descendants to full maturity and complete
> fellowship with God. In principle they can follow that road, but it will
> not be easy. They have inherited traits which enabled their ancestors to
> survive and to pass on their genes. And those traits will predispose them
> toward selfish behaviour and away from the kind of community – with
> God, one another, and creation – which God intends for them. Such
> behaviour is not 'hardwired' into them, but tendencies toward it are
> very strong . . . It is all too obvious that humanity has been in conflict
> from its beginnings. The biblical story indicates that this is an accurate
> *theological* description of what happened. The first humans took a wrong
> road, one 'that leads to destruction' (Mat 7:13), away from the goal that
> God intended . . . Purely secular history shows us that humanity has not
> known or worshiped the God of Israel and has been in conflict from
> its beginning. What the biblical story does is to provide a theological
> understanding of that history.[8]

------

6. The interplay of brain processes, behaviour and biblical understanding has been explored in depth in recent years. See: W. S. Brown, N. Murphy and H. N. Malony (eds.), *Whatever Happened to the Soul? Scientific and Theological Portraits of Human Nature* (Minneapolis: Fortress, 1998); M. A. Jeeves (ed.), *From Cells to Souls – And Beyond: Changing Portraits of Human Nature* (Grand Rapids: Eerdmans, 2004); Green, *Body, Soul,* n. 1, p. 110.

7. F. J. Ayala, 'Biological Evolution and Human Nature', in M. A. Jeeves (ed.), *Human Nature* (Edinburgh: Royal Society of Edinburgh, 2006), pp. 46–64.

8. Murphy, 'Roads to Paradise', n. 3, p. 115.

In 'Dover Beach' published in 1867, Matthew Arnold lamented the ebbing sea of faith:

> The Sea of Faith
> Was once, too, at the full, and round earth's shore
> Lay like the folds of a bright girdle furled.
> But now I only hear
> Its melancholy, long, withdrawing roar.

His pessimism is conventionally attributed to the ferment stirred by Darwin's ideas. Whilst it is certainly true that the *Origin of Species* provides a powerful formula for those wanting to evade the claims of the creating and redeeming God, it is wholly inaccurate to assume that it is the source for a universal acid which will destroy faith. Arnold's unease may have been focused by the *Origin*, but its roots are better seen in the general discomfort we all find in adjusting to any kind of change, despite living in a culture 'held together' by God's Son (Col. 1:17; Heb. 1:3). The challenge to us is the same as Arnold's. As we look at the world around us, are we able to see it as God's work?[9] The pioneering astronomer, Johannes Kepler, wrote to a friend, 'I wanted to become a theologian; for a long time I was unhappy. Now behold, God is praised by my work, even in astronomy.'[10] He saw his scientific studies as 'thinking God's thoughts after him'.

Questions about evolution trouble many Christians; they sadly obsess some. For some the way forward is in attacking Darwin. That is not our way. We read the Bible as attesting of a dynamic active God working through, although not confined by 'natural' processes; he is certainly infinitely more than a clever watchmaker

---

9. It can be argued that debates about evolution dangerously distract Christians from developing a robust doctrine of creation. This has been powerfully argued by Tom Wright in *New Heavens, New Earth*. (Cambridge: Grove Biblical Series B11, 1999), and in 'Jesus is coming – plant a tree' (*The Green Bible* [London: HarperCollins, 2008], pp. I: 73–85).

10. Letter to Michael Maestlin, 3 October 1595.

or an absentee landlord.[11] Darwin did not cause the sea of faith to ebb, because faith does not depend on knowing how the creator has worked. Rather, we would be better to remember Darwin for some words from Francis Bacon's *Advancement of Learning* which he inserted before the text proper of the *Origin*: 'Let no man think that he can search too far or be too well studied in the book of God's words or in the book of God's works; rather let all endeavour an endless proficience in both.' We unreservedly concur. Too many Christians fear that science will confuse or upset their understanding of God. We believe the psalmist chose the right way in declaring, 'Great are the works of the Lord; studied by all who delight in them' (Ps. 111:2). These words were carved on the doors of the Cavendish Laboratory (Physics Department) in Cambridge University when it was built in 1870s and also on the New Cavendish, opened in 1973.[12]

Augustine castigated the way that some Christians in his time interpreted Genesis. His criticisms are still pertinent:

> It is a disgraceful and dangerous thing for an infidel to hear a Christian presumably giving the meaning of Holy Scripture, talking nonsense on [matters of science]; and we should take all means to prevent such an embarrassing situation, in which people show up vast ignorance in a Christian and laugh it to scorn. The shame is not so much that an ignorant individual is derided, but that people outside the household of the faith think our sacred writers held such opinions, and, to the great

---

11. 'If reality contains nothing but quarks, leptons, and four interactions, then history is indeed filled with chance events and, as Dawkins and Dennett would have us believe, we are the result of a mindless process. If God exists, however, then other possibilities open up. Perhaps the unfolding of history includes a steady infusion of divine creativity under the scientific radar. Perhaps the meaning we encounter in so many places and so many different ways is not simply an accident of our biology, but a hint that the universe is more than particles and their interactions.' Karl Giberson, *Saving Darwin* (New York: HarperCollins, 2008), p. 220.

12. R. J. Berry, 'The Research Scientist's Psalm', *Science and Christian Belief* 20 (2008), pp. 147–161.

loss of those for whose salvation we toil, the writers of our Scripture
are criticised and rejected as unlearned men. If they find a Christian
mistaken in a field which they themselves know well and hear him
maintaining his foolish opinions about our books, how are they going to
believe those books in matters concerning the resurrection of the dead,
the hope of eternal life, and the kingdom of heaven, when they think
their pages are full of falsehoods on facts which they themselves have
learnt from experience and the light of reason?[13]

It is our conviction that there is no conflict between Holy
Scripture and modern science. Indeed the Christian doctrine of
creation provided the ground for the rise of science. The idea that
Christian faith and science are in conflict and always have been is
a myth propagated by Humanists for ideological reasons, but sadly
they are helped by sincere Christian believers who think they are
defending Holy Scripture when in fact they are doing no more
than defending *interpretations* of Holy Scripture which are sadly
inadequate. That does not mean to say that all the questions are
answered, all the problems settled and all the mysteries resolved.
That is never the case in either theology or natural science! Both
are ongoing quests for deeper understanding. But Christians who
are theologians and Christians who are scientists unite in confessing with John Calvin:

> The creation is quite like a spacious and splendid house, provided
> and filled with the most exquisite and the most abundant furnishings.
> Everything in it tells us of God.[14]

---

13. Augustine, *The Literal Meaning of Genesis*, transl. John Taylor (New York:
    Paulist Press, 1982), p. 43.
14. Institutes, 1: 4: 20

GENERAL INDEX